directing
in the
theatre

a casebook
Second Edition

j. robert wills

the scarecrow press, inc.
metuchen, n.j., & london
1994

An *Instructor's Manual* is available.

British Library Cataloguing-in-Publication data available

Library of Congress Cataloging-in-Publication Data

Wills, J. Robert, 1940-
    Directing in the theatre : a casebook / J. Robert Wills.—2nd
ed.
        p.   cm.
        ISBN 0-8108-2735-2 (alk. paper)
        1. Theater—Production and direction—Case studies.   I.
    Title.
    PN2053.W5   1994
    792'.0233—dc20   93-29274

for Barbara

Table of Contents

List of Cases

Preface to the Second Edition

This second edition of *Directing in the Theatre* includes an expanded array of materials for use in the study of directing. There are new cases about censorship, non-traditional casting, theatre safety, ethics, and other subjects of both current and enduring interest. The edition also features the introduction of "briefs," which are shortened, streamlined cases designed to stimulate discussion about such issues, among others, as gender in casting, auditions, giving and taking notes, learning lines, dealing with the public, and the establishment of company rules. These new materials have been added to the most effective cases from the previous edition, and the result is twice as much material as earlier. The number of cases has grown from twenty-two to forty-seven.

In addition, the entire collection has been completely reorganized. "The Director at Work" chapter has been enlarged to include both "Pre-Production" concerns and issues involved in "Casting and Rehearsals." A new chapter titled "Working with Actors" includes material about the individual actor, the problem scene, the ensemble, and performance inconsistency. Another new chapter, "Working with Other Collaborators," emphasizes the cooperative, nurturing nature of directing by examining the director at work with the stage manager, the lighting designer, the set designer, the playwright, the technicians and others. The final chapter, "Special Problems in Directing," has been expanded to include cases dealing with the large cast, evaluating the director's work, and presenting informal performances.

Mingled together throughout the book, these old and new cases affirm anew that every student can bring something of value to thoughtful classroom discussion. Because of this, they encourage collaborative learning in a community of peers, and they enable the instructor to serve as mentor, guide and facilitator in the development of individuals and groups. This means they also serve well the kind of active learning which has grown so much in importance during the last decade.

The additions and other changes presented here have roots in the students I have encountered in teaching and directing throughout the last decade. They may not see their work on every page, but it is there. Whether earlier at the University of Kentucky and the University of Texas at Austin, or now at Pacific Lutheran University, these students have nurtured my own learning, even as—I hope—they have learned themselves. Thanks, too, are due Mary Evans, who typed the new materials.

The original edition of the casebook has evidently served its users well for thirteen years. I hope this revised and expanded edition further enriches teaching and learning.

J. Robert Wills
1993

Preface to the First Edition

The case method of instruction, of course, is not new. It has long been used by several diverse academic disciplines, and its pedagogical effectiveness can be well documented. But using the case method in theatre *is* new. In fact, this book provides the first body of cases available for such use. Because of this, these pages should offer a lively and stimulating addition to the teaching and learning of directing for the theatre.

At its simplest, a case is a description of a problem or situation halted at a point where decisions must be made. Students study a case, come to individual decisions about it, then join together for discussion and debate of the issues presented in the case material. In other words, there are two important elements at work in using the case method. First, there is the case material itself. And second, there is the classroom discussion that results from that material.

When students in directing confront a series of cases, they reach out again and again to meet real problems actually faced by a director in the theatre. What they learn from such confrontation can then be transferred to their own directing experiences. Meanwhile, their learning is active and situational rather than passive and isolated. They learn to *use* knowledge by applying it to specific situations, and by testing their insights against the insights of peers.

The method demands discipline, attention to facts and high levels of interaction, especially between student and student. The instructor acts more as a catalyst, guide and summarizer than as a giver of information.

The method also demands understanding and accepting that in any given situation there are multiple possibilities for action. There are no "correct" answers to the issues raised in cases, for rarely is there only one appropriate way to solve a problem or only one artistic decision that will work. Consequently, case discussion infrequently results in unanimity of opinion. Nor should that be a goal. Rather, each participant in the discussion must be ready to defend his or her own judgment against the total experience of all who participate. In this way the case method helps students learn how to explore the alternatives before deciding what to do. It also helps them understand that logic has limitations.

The cast method of teaching and learning, then, focuses on problems, not techniques, and brings field experience in the theatre directly to the classroom. It's learning by doing, without having to live with the consequences. All participants possess the same materials and information, to which they bring uniquely individual viewpoints, and from which they must be prepared to recommend wise and appropriate action.

The cases presented here can be used at any level of study, from beginning to advanced. Furthermore, they can be used alone or in conjunction with any current directing textbook or other course materials. They can also be an effective adjunct to actual laboratory experience, to apprenticeship or to lecture presentations. Indeed, it is precisely this amazing flexibility which enables the case method to add to the arsenal of teaching tools and techniques for directing.

Classroom tested over a three-year period, the cases included in this volume encompass a wide range of theatre settings—from off Broadway, to college and university theatres, to community theatres and secondary school theatres. Even resident theatres and dinner theatres make an appearance. Only rarely, however, are the problems which confront the director unique to a specific type of theatre situation. More often, there is common ground which binds directors together regardless of the environment in which they work.

In like manner, the range of directing problems confronted in these cases is also wide. Though no pretense can be given to total completeness, the cases touch virtually every major area of importance to the director, from the initial confrontation with a script to problems that arise in performance. In addition, most of the cases can be approached successfully with many different emphases. Consequently, the questions included are intended only to be points of departure. They should be augmented, enlarged and changed according to need.

In difficulty, the cases presented here range from the fairly detailed and comprehensive (much in the pattern of those used frequently in business administration) to the more informal and shorter, similar to those popular in library science. Regardless of detail or length, however, each case is based on a real situation actually faced by a director in the theatre. More often than not, the names, places, theatres, and sometimes even the plays themselves have been disguised. Sometimes two or more experiences which involved similar problems have been combined into one case. The result is fictionalized history, where emphasis can be on problems and issues rather than on identification of a specific situation. In their present form, therefore, the cases are intended for classroom use only. They were developed as vehicles for instruction and discussion rather than as examples of either effective or ineffective handling of directing situations.

As can be guessed, the case materials have been drawn from many sources. Some sprang from my own experience in a variety of settings. Some have been derived in part from published sources. Still others have come from interviews and case research with other directors active in the field. I am particularly grateful to people like James T. and Carol S. Cleveland, Charles David Haller, Douglas and Deborah Powell, Marita Woodruff and several others who willingly and eagerly shared their directing experiences with me and then read the resulting cases to insure their accuracy and focus.

Finally, thanks are due to Jane Schnelle and Wini Humphrey, who typed the many different versions of each case, including the final copy.

I am convinced that teaching and learning can always be improved. I'm also convinced that the case method offers one viable alternative towards that improvement. These specific cases, then, are offered to students and teachers of theatre in the hope of testing those two premises.

J. Robert Wills
1980

Introduction: Learning Through the Case Method
(A Note for Students)

This book has a single purpose: to help students learn about directing.

Yet the book is neither a manual of practical suggestions nor a philosophical treatise. It's not even a textbook in the usual sense. Rather, it's a casebook. It contains nothing but cases.

Consequently, it will present a new experience for most students of theatre, and since any new experience quite naturally carries with it questions about the unknown, those students may rightfully wonder just what to expect. Therefore, some explanation may prove useful at the beginning, to help insure that everyone understands what the case method is, and to suggest some specific ways for the experience of studying cases to be as valuable as possible.

Such explanation is the purpose of this Introduction. It contains a brief statement about cases and the case method. It also suggests how case study relates to directing. Then, after reviewing the values of case study, it offers some very specific suggestions for case preparation and discussion.

What Is a Case?

Those who have read the Prefaces to this book will recall that a case, at its simplest, is a description of a problem or situation halted at a point where decisions must be made. It's more than an example, more than a hypothetical slice of life, certainly more than a mere riddle. It's a factual account of prior events, presented as objectively as possible.

In other words, a case presents a *real* situation, one actually faced by a director in theatre. More often than not, it sees

1

things as the director saw them, so is filled with all the data and opinions and people which the director confronted. Each case is a short historical story of sorts, a narrative record of something which happened in the past.

A "brief" is also a case. It, too, presents a real situation. Usually, however, the brief is short (and the play on words is both deliberate and obvious), not long, so it presents a concise, summarized account rather than a fully detailed narration. In this sense, briefs are abstracts, and they sometimes go beyond describing specific directing situations to raise questions about the nature and practice of directing itself. Like their longer counterparts, the brief is based on reality, on something that really happened.

Regardless of this factual base, however, and regardless of whether it is long or short, a case stands more as an invitation than as a work of historical literature. It bids students to face the reconstruction of a specific directing experience as if it were theirs, to analyze the situation, and then to recommend a responsible course of action for solving whatever problems seem to exist. In this way a case represents field experience brought to the classroom. It invites students to experience the problems, joys and processes of directing—during which people, things, ideas, events, goals and attitudes come together at points where there is a problem, or where something needs to be resolved.

What Is the Case Method?

Actually, there is no such thing as *the* case method. Instead, there are many methods, for what happens in the study of cases depends not only on the case material itself, but even more on the individual students and instructors who use the case material. It's the chemistry of a specific learning environment that makes cases come alive, and such chemistry changes from classroom to classroom, from student to student, from teacher to teacher. Consequently, there are many different ways in which case study can be effective. There is no one magic formula, no single prescription that must be followed.

Within this wide latitude for individual differences, however, the case method of learning does have a distinguishing, if simple, characteristic. It is nothing more (and nothing less) than a process in which students confront a series of cases—several rather than just one—so they face the repeated and collective experience of reaching out to solve problems and make decisions. The multiple cases provide a framework for learning, a system in education that has proved valuable for over a hundred years.

Mildred Hawksworth Lowell describes the method concisely in *The Management of Libraries and Information Centers,* Vols. I–IV (Scarecrow Press, Metuchen, NJ, 1968). "The case method," she says, "is a philosophy of education; it can be defined as the utilization of cases in studying and analyzing problems upon which the practice of a profession rests. Essentially, it is a project or laboratory method in that the student not only studies source material, but also applies the principles derived from this study to the activities that are a part of the practical preparation for his profession."*

The method began at the Harvard Law School early in the 1870's; it has since spread to such diverse fields as business, social work, physical education, library science and human relations, among others. Wherever used, it has met with positive results, adding well to the other various methods by which people learn.

What's Important About Directing?

Any complete response to this question, of course, will fill many pages, but one brief answer can be found in Hugh Hunt's *The Director in the Theatre* (London, 1954). Hunt says, "The theatre, like all the arts, is more easily analyzed by practice than by theory, and what we see when we go to it, and when we act in it, is of infinitely greater value than what we can say or write of it. Yet for all its mystique, its emotions, its ephemeral existence, the play on stage is nine-tenths a matter of craftsmanship, planning and clear-thinking."

---

* Volume I: The Case Method in Teaching Library Management, p. 27.

Case study will not lead necessarily to development of Hunt's unmentioned one-tenth—to greater magic, mystique and vision, to the creative intellect which every director must develop and use. Nor will it contribute directly to increased skills in the sheer craftsmanship demanded for directorial excellence. Both vision and craft lie outside its direct purview.

On the other hand, case study can add significantly to what Hunt calls "planning" and "clear-thinking," and it can do this, primarily, because it provides vicarious experience in the process of directing at its central moments, and because it provides entry into the practice of confronting specific directing problems. To quote the Harvard University Catalogue for the Law School, "the case method is a realistic method which uses the careful examination of directing precedent as a focus for study and as a starting point for classroom discussion. The case method introduces the student to the analytical techniques which directors use to sort the relevant from the irrelevant, separate reasoning from rationalization, and distinguish solid principle from speculation."

To state the obvious, there's a big difference between talking about directing in the classroom and actually directing in a theatre. It's the difference between theory and practice, between imagining a play in the mind's eye and making that same play come alive on stage. And, as everyone knows, the leap from one to the other can frequently prove difficult—for the experienced director as well as for the novice.

Case study can help bridge that gap. While it fails to provide an equal substitute for first-hand experience, it does, outside of actually directing, provide the closest possible approximation to understanding what directors face as they go about their work, and it enables students to confront those same situations with creative rigor and intellectual discipline. Case study of directing makes other learning more meaningful because it lets students apply concepts and theories to concrete situations. It demands total integration of knowledge, which then transfers well to the actual practice of directing. It also frequently pushes students to develop their own views and beliefs about directing, and thereby helps them to establish their own artistic voices.

Student Response to Case Study

Students in recent years have found the case method to be both valuable and exciting. In fact, their written evaluations, submitted after experience with anywhere from twelve to twenty-five individual cases in a given semester, may suggest to other students just how great the rewards can be. Here is what nine of them have said.

"The case method forced me to think, to use my knowledge in specific ways. It also encouraged my normal curiosity. I've grown more in the past fifteen weeks than ever before."

"I feel the cases contributed more to my learning (that is, to my real knowledge about directing) than any other part of the course."

"This class was totally different from any I have ever taken before, and the reasoning used was something I hadn't ever tried. I found a different part of my brain opened up. What was most exciting was many times my own conclusions were changed completely by the class discussion and probing."

"I was exposed to broad but intricate problems, all of which increased my respect for directing. Many times throughout the semester I felt frustrated: we weren't actually solving the problems presented. Or at least we weren't agreeing on the solutions. Now I realize the unanswered questions should remain that way. As an individual I should sort them out in my own way, according to my own values. Luckily, this course has helped me realize and come to a better understanding of those values."

"Experience is the best teacher, they say, and the case method gave us 'real' experience, but within friendly boundaries."

"Interesting, stimulating, challenging—very useful method. It stimulated class discussion better than anything I had ever experienced before."

"I enjoyed it and the cases were very interesting. No matter how simple they appeared at first, they all became fun to discuss."

"All I can say is that two and a half hours are not long enough to do this method justice. When I think of the fifty-minute classes that bore me to tears, and this class which kept my interest for over twice that long, I can't help but believe firmly that this is the best way to learn."

"The effort of confronting a problem and analyzing a case, followed by extensive discussion, made learning more solid than just any 'sit-and-take notes' class. I had to think, question, doubt, reaffirm. And that's good."

These comments are not intended as testimonials, nor do they represent all the student opinion generated. Rather, they demonstrate one range of positive response to the reality of case study. They also begin to suggest the values that can arise from case learning, values that every student can anticipate.

Luckily, even while demanding, case study is fairly straight-forward. Students need only recognize the need for discipline, for careful preparation, for cooperative interaction with fellow students and for individual responsibility in solving problems. Having fulfilled these obligations, the rewards should be great.

Values of the Case Method

In one sense, case study is highly practical, so its values derive primarily from the increased ability to act wisely in a given situation, an ability that transfers well from classroom to stage. In another sense, case study is highly theoretical, so its values derive primarily from an increased ability to think, especially an ability to think in ways which can effectively serve the working director. It's this relationship between thinking and doing, between the practical and theoretical, which makes the case method so useful in studying directing.

Then, too, directors never use knowledge in a vacuum. It's not enough for them merely to memorize rules or master elements of craft. It's not even enough just to think great thoughts or have inspired vision. On the contrary, directors need the analytical skill to use information when it's needed.

In directing, the rules, craft, thought and vision must be translated into performance, usually through the detailed and steady process of preparation. Case study can help ease this translation so that it becomes more effective.

Andrew R. Towl wrote *To Study Administration by Cases* (Boston, 1969), and what he says about business administration holds equally true for theatre: "Many different types of courses properly belong in a curriculum designed for different groups of students," he said, "but objectives must be carefully considered. Surely, if the purpose is only to communicate a body of information a well-organized text or program of learning may well be the most efficient method. If the purpose, however, is to develop capacity to use information at the point of decision, the sequential acquisition of knowledge must be converted to make it available for random access at the moment of need. Students who have had to reach out for information in arriving at decision after decision in a series of cases have been able to recall and utilize information effectively when applicable in new situations or to seek new information when it becomes relevant."

In a similar manner, students who are asked to reach toward their innermost selves in response to questions like "What would *you* do in this situation?" or "What do you think about these ideas?" are apt to discover and develop their own uniquenesses as artists. They are not only learning about directing; they are learning about themselves.

Learning to think, learning to act wisely, learning to use knowledge in making effective decisions, learning to know one's self—these are the principal values which spring from case study in directing.

Yet students of directing can also benefit from case study in other ways as well, and it may be useful to review a "shopping list" of what those other values are. The listing which follows appears in random order and is meant to be suggestive rather than exhaustive; it also depends on the reader to provide important and overlapping relationships.

1. Case study aids in developing judgment and understanding, two qualities of vast importance for the director in theatre. Certainly they affect everything from script selection

and analysis to handling emergencies that arise in performance. Some would argue, in fact, that quality of judgment is the director's most important asset.

2. Case study involves students *in* a situation (at its critical moments) rather than just asking them to theorize *about* a situation. It is a "you are there" approach to learning, with the significant advantage of time for reflection. The opposite disadvantage, of course, is that students don't have to live with the consequences of their decisions.

3. Case study enables students to participate in many different experiences in a limited amount of time. To direct twelve different plays, for example, in a given semester might prove impossible. To study twelve cases, however, is not.

4. Case study offers learning that is active rather than passive. It encourages student involvement. It commands attention. It treats students as participants in education rather than as consumers of information.

5. Case study enables students to learn from one another as well as from the teacher. It lets them test ideas among peers.

6. Case study encourages recognition of common problems. Directors, regardless of the specific situation in which they find themselves, frequently face similar issues and quandaries. Case study provides a reservoir for shared experience, and enables students to learn from directors who have preceded them.

7. Case study involves students and teacher in shared discovery. There are no perfect solutions, no answers in the back of the book, no experts to issue final declarations. Only mutual effort leads to understanding. Some students find this lack of finality awkward at first; most soon realize that virtually every problem can be approached in several different, equally effective ways.

8. Case study generates student interest and enthusiasm, partly because of the case material itself, partly because of the interplay introduced by discussion. As educational theorists know, high interest levels generate higher levels of learning.

9. Case study helps students know what they don't know. It also helps them know that what they don't know is important. Everyone lacks sufficient knowledge at one time

or another, and rarely do directors have all the information they might desire. Recognition of this fact, coupled with the ability to search out information when it is needed, adds to a director's effectiveness.

10. Case study increases ability in interpersonal relations, an ability that not only enhances case discussion, but also provides a direct carryover to interacting with co-workers in the theatre. After all, directors spend most of their time in a human relations endeavor, trying to motivate, shape and sustain positive change in others.

11. Case study provides immediate feedback on ideas. There's no waiting for the return of examinations or reports, no saving questions until after class. What students think becomes instant substance for analysis and discussion.

12. Case study suggests that logic has limitations, that directors must often use what's known only as preparation to leap into the unknown. It helps increase the quality of intuition, one human ability no good director can live without.

13. Case study focuses more on the process of directing than on the product. It's very concerned with how and why things happen, with the director as a creator of change.

14. Case study places responsibility for learning directly on students. Nothing will happen without their preparation and participation. In fact, both the quantity and quality of learning depends on their willingness to assume responsibility for what happens in the classroom.

15. Case study helps students focus on problems, not just on techniques or theories. Too often the "tools" of directing are isolated from the situation which affects their use. Case study breaks down this isolation, forces students to use their growing skills to address concrete issues. It develops "situational thinking."

16. Case study encourages a holistic approach to directing. It enables students to examine the process of directing as a total system in which all parts are related, in which change in one area is likely to have a ripple effect elsewhere. Thus, case study provides a truer portrait of directing than does isolated study of the individual skills involved.

17. Case study demands that a student's total life experience become grist for the case. The case material itself

provides a focal point, but its study and analysis will vary greatly from student to student. As with several persons who have seen an automobile accident, attitudes, beliefs, even facts will change according to individual perceptions. Students bring everything they are to case study and discussion.

18. Case study emphasizes knowledge, suggests that the role of knowledge can never be underestimated. The more students know, the more they can bring to each individual case. Thus, case study can proceed on many different levels, depending on the backgrounds of those who are involved. A case discussion during the first week of a semester should be different from discussion of the same case later in the year. In like manner, discussion by sophomores should differ from discussion by advanced graduate students.

19. Case study helps establish attitudes and skills which can be useful in directing, especially the notion that theatre works best as a cooperative venture. (As one outstanding costumer maintains with regularity, "Theatre is just another team sport.") Case study, like theatre itself, also magnifies the role of individual achievement within the group effort.

Thus, the values of case study can be far ranging. Yet there are also many things that case study will not accomplish. For this reason, it should be viewed as an additional tool for learning, not as a replacement for something else. It can exist side by side with reading, lectures, exercises, examinations, laboratory experience, apprenticeship, research papers and all the other useful techniques for education and training.

Unluckily, like all the teaching and learning methods combined, case study will not automatically make one a better director. Whatever magic that demands has yet to be discovered. Case study can, however, help one *think* more like a director, thus preparing the way for directing itself to be of higher quality.

Case Preparation

How, then, can students gain most from the case method? They must begin, of course, by devising effective ways to approach and study individual cases—a process known as case preparation. The best ways for any individual will evolve with experience. Surely there is no one best way. In fact, it can be argued that every student will eventually contrive a unique method, one that works best within his or her own special framework. Nevertheless, some generalized suggestions are possible, and may prove especially helpful at the beginning.

1. Read the case carefully.

2. Then, as Tyrone Guthrie suggested a director should do for a play, read it "again and again and again and again—and again."

3. Try to get the "feel" of the situation. In what kind of environment is the director working? What are the formal and informal pressures affecting the situation?

4. Examine the evidence as presented. Be open to it, receptive to its implications. (Some cases, of course, present more evidence than others.)

5. Guard against the impulse to invent what doesn't exist. Deal with the material actually presented in the case.

6. Remember that directors never have all the information they need; instead, they must deal somehow with the information they do have. They may also ask what additional information is needed, though often it may be unavailable.

7. Separate fact from opinion. Value each for what it is—and for what it is not.

8. Make margin notes; underline important items; circle key words or phrases; draw arrows back and forth—use your pencil in every way that will help you remember and identify elements in the case.

9. Guard against your own assumptions. See the case on its own grounds.

10. Use the questions provided at the end of each case to begin your thinking about the case. Make notes in response to them.

11. Don't limit your response just to these questions. Ask yourself, What other questions should be asked?

12. Identify the problems involved and the reasons for the problems. In certain cases, the problems will be more obscure than in others. In other cases, what seem at first to be

problems may only be symptoms. The director, like the medical internist, must be an excellent diagnostician.

13. Remember that a case brings together not only facts, but also people, ideas, opinions, prejudices, traditions—and the whole host of other elements that influence human behavior, whether in or out of theatre.

14. Once you have identified and analyzed the problems involved, begin to search for possible solutions.

15. Consider as many alternative solutions as you can think of. Don't limit yourself only to one option, or even only to two. Guard especially against seeing the case as an either/or proposition.

16. Consider the implications and consequences of each of your options.

17. Make a decision. Which option—or options—seems best (most appropriate) for the case?

18. Decide how you would implement your decision. How would you carry it out effectively?

19. Ask yourself, what will be the results of this action? What other things might happen because of what you do?

20. Be creative in your thinking. Don't settle only for solutions that are known or that worked for other directors in the past. Just as directors must often create craft, they must also seek new solutions to old problems.

Following these suggestions should provide for adequate initial case preparation. Each student, too, will discover additional steps which can be helpful. Some will use exhaustive margin notes. Others will prepare reams of accompanying analyses. Still others will use note cards, identifying different areas of concern on different cards. What's important is to discover a coherent system for preparation, coupled with a system for recalling that preparation when in class.

Actually, the twenty suggestions listed above fall often into six separate steps, each of which shares equal importance for case preparation. The steps are these:

1. Identify the problem(s) or issue(s) involved in the case.
2. Identify the causes or reasons for the problem.
3. Determine alternative ways to deal with the problem.

4. Select what seems to be the best of those alternatives.

5. Devise a plan for implementing whatever decisions have been made.

6. Evaluate the implementation process and its likely consequences.

Some of the "briefs" short-circuit these six specific steps; they ask students, not to identify and determine the cause for problems, but to address issues clearly identified in the case, and to address those issues in ways which amplify them, limit them or otherwise relate them to specifically stated goals. In some ways, these cases may appear less complex at first glance. In reality, they may turn out to be the most complicated, because their discussion relies more on the accumulated knowledge and insight of class members than on the specific details of case history. These cases, too, take careful preparation. They demand, too, the consideration of options, the making of choices and the justification of decisions.

How much time will all this take? That's a difficult question to answer, of course, and it will vary somewhat from student to student. Certainly more time is demanded than would be involved in only a cursory reading of each case. Certainly, also, as depth of insight increases, so does case preparation time. The converse is equally true: as case preparation time increases, so does depth of insight.

Case Discussion

Adequate case preparation, regardless of how thorough, is only half a solution to the effective use of cases. Students also need to be effective participants in case discussion, that coming together to share ideas with colleagues and peers. As with preparation, discussion abilities will evolve with experience, and roles will change continuously in the give-and-take of a specific group of people, but the following suggestions may help at the beginning.

1. Remember that what you bring to the discussion will be different from what others bring. Your skills, knowledge,

attitudes, past experience, prejudices, insights, wisdom—all are unique. No one else will see the case quite like you do. This can lead to some surprising differences of opinion, and to the sure knowledge that no student ever manages to think of everything that is involved in a given case.

2. Be ready to advance your own ideas. Don't fall into the trap of just responding to what someone else thinks.

3. Listen. Carefully. Critically.

4. Ask questions.

5. If you don't understand something someone says, say so. Ask for a further explanation.

6. State your disagreements (and agreements) freely.

7. Accept freely any disagreement with or criticism of your own ideas. But also be ready to defend your opinion and to explain why you believe what you do.

8. Be ready to change your mind, if that seems called for and if you are convinced by someone else's line of reasoning.

9. Deal with the case. Remember, you never have all the information you might wish you had. Others in the discussion don't have it either.

10. Use your prepared notes, margin comments, written analyses, etc., to help focus your thoughts.

11. Be clear and succinct. Learn how to speak to the point. No one likes long, rambling statements that seem to have nothing to do with anything.

12. Don't monopolize the conversation. Neither be forever silent. Cases demand cooperative discussion, give-and-take among many participants.

13. Build on ideas and thoughts under review. Know when you're changing the subject.

14. Help to establish an open atmosphere in which everyone can participate freely and without inhibition, in which ideas can be examined rigorously, but without malice.

15. If you find yourself stuck, or at a loss for words, or in the midst of an awkwardly stated thought, rely on fellow students to assist you. Ask for help.

16. Be yourself. Don't play an assumed role. Like directors, creative discussion participants work in individual ways for the common good.

17. Be prepared for a lack of finality. Case discussions

often end neither in unanimity nor consensus, which is fine. More often than not, there is no one absolutely best solution to any problem.

18. Realize that no one, including your instructor, has *the* answer to a case problem.

Conclusion

You should now be ready to tackle case study—and to enjoy the process which lies ahead. If you take the cases at their face value, if you prepare adequately and participate effectively in discussions, if you are open to alternatives, if you are willing to disagree and face disagreement, if you make decisions responsibly and with awareness for their consequences, then you should gain all the benefits that case study can offer. You'll also be an active participant in your own education.

Chapter I   The Director: An Overview

CASE 1. *THE MADMAN AND THE NUN*

William Keller had endured three weeks of rehearsal as director of the Springton Community Theatre (SCT) production of *The Madman and the Nun,* during which time the lack of cooperation in his cast, the absence of administrative or technical support, and the literal desertion by the SCT Board of Directors had driven him to despair. Two weeks remained before the production was scheduled to open, but Keller wasn't sure he could continue as director. He thought it might be better to resign, to let the play be cancelled—or be salvaged by someone else. There seemed little hope of change.

The Springton Community Theatre

The only community theatre in Springton, Indiana, the SCT had been producing plays for more than forty years, during which time it had experienced all the peaks and valleys typical of a volunteer arts organization. It had never generated a large audience following, a broad base of economic support, or an abundance of active participants. Yet each year a shifting core of six to ten dedicated, hardworking people—augmented by an increasingly small number of others—managed to organize and present a season of five or six plays. Most of this dedicated core soon found themselves elected to SCT's Board of Directors, an informally constituted body charged with artistic, fiscal and administrative leadership for the theatre. The Board met regularly only once each year, as required by its charter. The day-to-day activity was carried out by those members who assumed leadership roles at various times throughout the year.

The SCT enjoyed a precarious financial existence, one that depended entirely on limited and unpredictable box-office income. Furthermore, the Board had not encouraged the discovery of other income sources. In fact, just one year before *The Madman and the Nun,* the theatre had refused an "artistic assistance" grant from the state arts council. (The grant would have provided 90 percent of the salary and fringe benefits needed to employ a combination artistic director and business manager.) The theatre did, however, have its own

18

building, a one-hundred-fifty-seat theatre within a renovated nineteenth-century mansion, which it rented in perpetuity from a local foundation for ten dollars a year.

A play selection committee, elected from among the Board of Directors, chose plays to be presented each year. A director selection committee, also elected from the Board, chose a director to stage each production. Interested persons were invited to submit the names of plays and directors for consideration, and only rarely were either selected very far in advance. Once selected, the director served also as the producer, assuming responsibility for all aspects of the production. Auditions, though rarely well attended, were open to all interested persons in the community. Technical crews were recruited from community volunteers. No one, of course, including the directors, received any financial compensation.

The 1983–84 season for the SCT had begun with Arthur Miller's *The Price,* followed by Neil Simon's *Barefoot in the Park,* Jean Kerr's *Mary, Mary* and Kaufman and Hart's *The Man Who Came to Dinner.* Each production had been mounted with difficulty and had run for five nights. Average attendance for each individual performance had been thirty-nine.

Board members approach Keller

Late in April, just before *The Man Who Came to Dinner* opened, several members of the Board of Directors—Lange Allger, Sue Biller and Mr. and Mrs. Ed Simpson—approached William Keller, asking if he would direct the final play of the season, to be staged early in June. The Director of Theatre at a local college, Dr. Keller had lived and taught in Springton for eleven years, but had never worked for the SCT. He had, however, built an active and strong liberal arts theatre program on campus and was known in the community as an excellent director. (The college theatre and the SCT were the only producing theatres in town.)

The Board members, each of whom Keller knew and respected, appealed to him for several reasons. They thought having a knowledgeable and skilled director, even for a single production, could help improve the entire SCT program. They also thought Keller's presence would add a level of competence to what they freely admitted had been a floundering year. They were the core, they argued to Keller, of a small group that hoped to make the SCT a more reputable theatre, one whose stature could begin to grow within the community. Furthermore, if he agreed to direct, they said, he could be assured that each of them—plus others they would influence—would audition for the production, thus assuring him of an adequate cast.

At first, Keller refused. His college schedule kept him far too busy to assume such a responsibility off campus. Furthermore, he had no desire to become affiliated with the continuing problems of the SCT. After listening to promises of Board support, however, and after considering the opportunity to direct in a new situation with non-student actors, he finally agreed.

Keller suggested to the Board members who had approached him that the theatre stage Stanislaw Witkiewicz's innovative and grotesque *The Madman and the Nun,* an early twentieth-century Polish play portrayed by one scholar as "difficult to describe because it is composed of such disparate elements, and suggests so much that it defies logical explanation." It was a play he had wanted to direct for some time, and he thought it might provide a new experience for the SCT audience. Allger, Biller and the Simpsons discussed the choice with the play selection committee. Everyone agreed that the play represented a dramatic change for the theatre; they also agreed the change could be beneficial and could begin to point a new direction for the organization. Consequently, the play selection committee agreed to the production.

Allger, Biller and the Simpsons offered to help in every possible way. They also agreed to encourage other Board members to help. Thus assured of continuing support, Keller began to prepare for the production.

The production

Auditions were announced through the usual channels: newspaper notices, calendar listings, direct mail and public service announcements on radio and television. By the time auditions arrived, Allger had moved from Springton and the Simpsons and Biller had decided they could not, after all, audition. The play, they explained, just seemed too extreme for them. Nevertheless, enough interested people did show up, and Keller cast the production without real difficulty. All except two of the eight actors were inexperienced.

The two experienced actors, Mary Ann and Charles Andrews, had never worked with the SCT, but they had acted extensively for four years in a dinner theatre only thirty miles away and, before that, while they were students at the nearby state university. Both had also performed on local television and in several state-produced tourism films. In 1982 they had attempted to form their own theatre in Springton, an effort that collapsed after two small productions. Keller knew they had shared a reputation for being troublemakers in their previous work, and while he did not want to use them, he felt there were no real alternatives. He could not deny their talent, and they seemed almost perfectly suited to play the two title roles. For their part, the Andrewses had become increasingly interested in experimental theatre. They auditioned for *The Madman and the Nun* solely because of their eagerness to perform in the Witkiewicz play.

Keller called a first rehearsal early in May. When everyone had arrived, Mary Ann Andrews asked if she could say something before rehearsal began. Keller agreed, and she launched into an elongated lecture about the nature of theatre and art, about the role of the actor and the director as actors prepare for performance, and about the necessity for experimentation in the modern theatre. Occasionally, Charles, her husband, interrupted to augment her comments. Several times Keller tried politely to bring the comments to a close, but without success. "What is she doing?" he wondered. After forty-five minutes Mary Ann turned to him and said, "Thank you. We can start now."

After the cast had read through the script, Keller began to talk with them about the production schedule. When he mentioned a date, two weeks in the future, by which time lines were to be memorized, Charles interrupted him, suggesting that memorization of lines was an outdated concept for the theatre. Directors, he argued, who used such role techniques were also outdated and shouldn't be allowed to direct. Keller responded by saying that, after all, Witkiewicz had written the words and it seemed only reasonable that actors acting the play should learn them. As he spoke, he noticed the rest of the cast was growing more and more confused by the evening's events. When rehearsal finally ended, Keller concluded that, all in all, it had been a disastrous beginning, one in which he had been able to exert very little influence or control.

Each night for the next week the Andrewses remained uncooperative and argumentative. While always polite and outwardly very pleasant, they questioned everything Keller suggested, implying by innuendo that their qualifications were so obviously superior that he should resign as director and turn the production over to them. Keller grew increasingly angry, but avoided any direct confrontation while he tried to keep the rest of the cast working effectively toward performance.

Keller also faced other problems. Each night during the first week actor Randy Little, a local high school student, showed up for rehearsals high on drugs. After talking with him two or three times about the issue, Keller finally voiced an ultimatum: "Either get rid of the junk or hand in the script. You cannot go on like this, simply because it's no good for you and certainly no good for the production. An actor can't afford to be stoned, to be out of control." Without hesitation, Randy turned in his script and walked away from rehearsal.

Keller replaced him the next day with one of his own students.

Keller's problems during this initial stage of production were not limited to the cast or to rehearsal. The community volunteer who had agreed to help with scenery left town for a month's vacation, apologizing for not being able to fulfill his responsibility. Neither Keller nor anyone on the theatre's Board of Directors could find someone to continue the job. Most of the usual theatre volunteers just weren't interested; some were busy with other community activities. Keller finally convinced a college colleague to design the set, then asked one of his regular students to oversee building it. The student had worked alone every day during the first week of rehearsal. No one from the theatre had been available to help.

As rehearsals progressed, the Andrewses accepted direction with growing belligerence. Often they simply ignored Keller, doing as they pleased and encouraging other cast members to follow their direction. By the middle of the third week, four days after lines were due, Charles still hadn't begun to memorize, though everyone else in the cast was off book. He was also still saying that he wouldn't, that he preferred to improvise around the meaning he would eventually discover.

Keller, knowing of no possible replacement for either Charles or Mary Ann, continued to rehearse as best he could. "I will not let them run me out," he said to himself.

On numerous occasions during these three weeks Keller spoke with members of the Board about the developing problems. He sought out especially the Simpsons. (Biller had begun a vacation and was unavailable.) They offered sympathy, saying how sorry they were that everything seemed to be going poorly. They also, for various reasons that Keller never fully understood, lamented their inability to do anything to help. As Mrs. Simpson had put into words: "Just keep doing the best you can. It will all work out. We always have problems like this." She also pointed out that Keller hadn't really started publicity for the production yet.

By the end of the third week Keller had reached the limits of his patience and had concluded that the easiest solution for the multiple dilemmas was for him to resign as director. Yet his sense of responsibility and his loyalty to the principles of theatre argued against quitting, as did his sense that Springton needed a good community theatre, which it would never have unless people like him tried to improve it. In addition, a streak of stubborn pride argued against giving in to the Andrewses. It would mean admitting defeat.

Questions

1. What problems, if any, does this case represent?

2. What could Keller have done to avoid the problems?

3. As Keller, what would you do now?

CASE 2. *PETER PAN*

Joan Liddy say quietly at her office desk, both puzzled and upset. As director of the Midwest University Theatre production of *Peter Pan* she had been charged with artistic and organizational responsibility for the play, which was scheduled to open in ten days. Yet two hours earlier one of the most crucial performers, Ann Dale, had announced she would miss six of the final ten rehearsals because of other commitments.

Liddy knew that Dale's missing so many rehearsals would have a devastating effect on the production. Cast morale was already low, as was cast discipline, and to have any single actor miss so much in the final week seemed unthinkable. She thought about replacing Dale or actually eliminating the role. Dale, however, was the lead dancer in a chorus of dancers whose presence had become integral to most of the play; six Indians, six pirates, six lost boys and four animals formed a dance ensemble of twenty-two dancers, among whom Dale moved as the single coordinating dancer. Eliminating her role, therefore, would mean new choreography and blocking for virtually the entire production. Replacing her seemed equally impossible. Extremely talented, Dale's presence added measurably to the production's quality. Furthermore, no other dancers of equal talent were currently available within the department.

As Liddy pondered her possibilities, she regretted that so many other disruptive changes had been made in the production. From the beginning, it seemed, the play had been plagued with one crisis after another. Personnel changes, rehearsal conflicts and design problems had combined to give the production an atmosphere of frenetic disarray. In fact, cast and crew members had begun calling it *Peter Panic.*

Liddy was to meet Dale briefly just before rehearsal, and by then needed to decide what to do. Whatever she did, she thought, needed to smooth the production rather than add further disruption. It also needed to help assert her position of leadership, while insuring that the production grow in quality during its final rehearsals.

Background

Midwest University, a state-supported college with an enrollment of 40,000 students, had been offering bachelor's, master's and doctoral programs in theatre for forty years, and had recently inaugurated a seven-member graduate student acting company known as the Performing Ensemble Troupe (PET). Some 140 undergraduate theatre majors and 50 graduate students combined with a faculty of twelve to produce a series of six major productions annually, together with twelve M.F.A. studio productions and a series of one-acts. The major productions played for six performances each, over a single weekend, and had developed a deserved reputation for excellence within the University and regional community. Musicals played for eleven performances, over two long weekends.

The theatre's various programs were governed by a faculty and student Board of Directors, with the long-standing tradition that individual directors had complete authority and responsibility for the plays they were directing. The Director of Theatre served as producer for all productions. Directing one or more of the major productions was a privilege usually extended to no more than three faculty directors each season.

History of Peter Pan

Peter Pan had been chosen in August for production in April as one of the theatre's major productions. Auditions were slated for early March. Assistant Professor William Marsh had been selected to direct the play, with John Riggs as scenic designer, Mary Laurens as costumer, and Joan Liddy as choreographer. All four faculty members had worked on previous productions of the play at other theatres, and at first their widely varying past experience produced some difficulty; but after several conferences, each agreed that common ground could be discovered for a new production. Marsh, Laurens and Riggs had joined the Midwest theatre faculty four years earlier; Liddy was a first-year instructor in the Department of Dance.

Early in January three special studio productions were added to the schedule. Then *Company,* a musical which had been first performed before Christmas, was selected to appear as part of a national theatre festival in April. Consequently, auditions for *Peter Pan* were shifted to early February, in order to provide additional and more flexible rehearsal time in the midst of a busier production schedule than earlier anticipated. Although this decision was delayed until January 21, so the audition change lacked widespread publicity, *Peter Pan* was cast without difficulty. Forty-nine persons auditioned for the thirty-two acting and dancing roles.

During the first week of rehearsal, most of the actors were involved with *Company,* so Marsh and Liddy worked primarily with the dance ensemble, choreographing during that time most of the production. Unfortunately, by the end of the week, one dancer had come down with mononucleosis and had to leave the production. Liddy, with Marsh's assistance, recast the role and reblocked the dance sequences, changing choreography where necessary to suit the new dancer. One week later, a second dancer, dissatisfied with her role, quit the production, then dropped out of school. Liddy and Marsh repeated their earlier procedure of recasting and rechoreographing.

Three weeks after rehearsals had begun, two weeks into concentrated work with the actors, Marsh missed a week of rehearsal due to illness. During this time the actors were excused while Liddy worked with the dancers. Finally, Marsh was admitted to the hospital; he resigned from the production. Liddy argued successfully that she be designated director, a move approved by the Board of Directors and the Director of Theatre. No one knew she had no prior directing experience.

Liddy's first action as the new director was to suspend rehearsals for a week while she asked Laurens and Riggs to redesign the production to focus more completely on her ideas rather than on Marsh's. They agreed, and when the new design was finished rehearsals began again, moving from stage to a rehearsal studio in order for the construction crew to strike and rebuild the set.

One week later, fifteen days before the scheduled opening, Anne Morlin, a member of the PET who had been cast as Mrs. Darling told Liddy she was quitting the production. Morlin explained to the Director of Theatre, Robert Persha, that she was opposed to Liddy's concept of the play and dissatisfied with its poor quality, as well as with Liddy's unorganized, chaotic rehearsal periods. Persha however, refused to let her withdraw from the production; her contract with the department required her to perform in mainstage productions. Morlin then reported to Liddy she would continue in the role.

When Riggs discovered two days later that the revised setting would impede the needed "flying," he told Liddy that the scenery would need to be redesigned and rebuilt once again. Liddy refused to give up more time on the stage, so Riggs agreed that needed changes could wait until the final week. Once technical rehearsals had started, the crew played "Musical Walls" one afternoon and rearranged the set to suit the flying, a change which required only minor rebuilding.

Ann Dale

Ann Dale was a senior theatre major, an excellent black dancer who had auditioned primarily for the roles of Peter Pan or Tiger Lily. She had expressed both disappointment and antagonism when cast only in the dance chorus, but had become excited upon learning how important dance would be to the production. Her father, a prominent member of Midwest University's Board of Trustees, had in previous years written irate letters to the University President when Ann had not been cast in roles she thought appropriate. Each time the President had called the Director of Theatre, not to exert any influence, he said, but only to inform.

As an active campus personality, Ann had several interests outside the theatre, and soon after being cast in *Peter Pan* she became involved in a series of dance programs planned for black students during Black Awareness Week. An annual highlight for black students, Black Awareness Week was an event sponsored by the Black Student Union at Midwest. It was scheduled to end the night before *Peter Pan* opened.

Ann explained to Liddy that she would miss six of the final

ten rehearsals for *Peter Pan* because of these additional responsibilities. Liddy, checking the rehearsal schedule (see the Appendix of this case), discovered Dale would actually miss only four rehearsals. Of these, two were final dress rehearsals, one a special dance rehearsal.

Questions

1. What problems, if any, does this case present? How could the problems have been avoided?

2. What should Liddy tell Dale?

3. What else, if anything, should Liddy do to help the production during the last ten days of rehearsal?

CASE 2. APPENDIX

Final Rehearsal Schedule

PETER PAN

Sunday (7–10)	Act I: Total Cast
Monday (7–10)	Act II: Total Cast
Tuesday (7–10)	Problem Scenes (Actors as called)
Wednesday (4–8)	First Run-through (Total cast)
*Thursday (7–10)	Special Dance Rehearsal (Dancers only)
Friday (6–12)	Technical Rehearsal (On stage)
*Saturday (7–12)	Technical Rehearsal (On stage with costumes)
Sunday (4 p.m. curtain)	Tech/Dress (On stage)
*Monday (8 p.m.)	Dress Rehearsal (On stage)
*Tuesday (8 p.m.)	Final Dress Rehearsal (Preview audience)
Wednesday	Opening Night

---

*The rehearsals Dale will miss.

CASE 3. *HAPPY DAY*

As Deborah Crewl thought back over her first major directing experience, two or three incidents stood out as significantly unusual and she wondered in retrospect just how best she should have faced them. Each had seemed devastating at the time it occurred. Yet perhaps, she thought, that resulted only from her own inexperience. She resolved to think through the past situations once again. After all, she hoped to pursue a career teaching theatre, so learning from this experience seemed necessary if future directing responsibilities were to be more fulfilling.

Brief background

A senior English, Theatre and Education major at Ellenberg College in Idaho, Deborah Crewl was a straight-A student and an active, talented participant in the Ellenberg Theatre production program. She had acted in many productions, served on many crews, and had directed several one-act plays for the Studio Season, a series of informal productions presented at various times throughout the year. Her work in theatre had proved consistently excellent, and the theatre faculty were pleased that she had chosen to pursue a career in theatre by teaching and directing at the secondary level.

During the second semester of her senior year, after completing all the necessary coursework, Crewl was assigned student teaching responsibilities at West High School, one of two senior high schools in town. West High had a two-person theatre faculty, one of whom—Carl Elm—had graduated from Ellenberg at the end of Crewl's freshman year. An English major with limited theatre background, Elm was to be her supervising teacher. She had known him slightly when he was a student, but there had been no contact between them for three years, although he had seen her perform in several Ellenberg productions.

Dramatic activity at West was limited. Two or three evenings of theatre were produced each year by a small but enthusiastic drama club. Only a few classes were taught as part of the regular curriculum. Both Elm and his colleague, Robert

Felsey, had primary teaching responsibilities in English and speech, as would Crewl for her student teaching assignment.

Crewl's experience

Elm met with Crewl before the semester began to outline her duties and responsibilities. Consequently, on her first day as a student teacher she arrived at West prepared for seven classes, as planned. She had total responsibility for four classes during the day; in the three others, she observed and assisted Elm. (They had previously agreed that this pattern would continue throughout the semester.) At the end of the day, exhausted, she collapsed in the teachers' lounge with Lynn Ballow, a fellow student teacher. Just as she was ready to leave, Elm approached her, saying "Here's the script for *Happy Day*. Read it tonight. Try-outs are scheduled for tomorrow after school and you'll be directing it. It's part of your student teaching responsibility."

Crewl's first impulse had been to object. No one, she thought, could direct effectively with only one day of preparation. Furthermore, nothing had ever been said about production activity being part of her student teaching load. In fact, she had anticipated no contact at all with the producing theatre program at West. Yet she was eager to direct, and was also eager to have contact with students outside the classroom. In addition, she worried that any hesitancy might affect Elm's eventual evaluation of her total work—an evaluation that would become a part of her official academic record and serve as her first recommendation when she applied for teaching jobs. Consequently, she accepted the script, agreeing to direct the play.

Auditions for *Happy Day* had been announced a week earlier, so students knew the play would be produced, although they did not know until try-outs who would direct it. Almost a dozen people auditioned, and Crewl had little difficulty casting the play. Elm attended try-outs and influenced her decisions somewhat by his strong recommendation for certain actors.

Rehearsals began immediately. Crewl agreed reluctantly to follow the rehearsal pattern Elm suggested as "usual" for

West High: three hours each evening, five nights a week, for eight weeks. To her it seemed too long a rehearsal period for an hour-long play with a high school cast.

Happy Day had four characters: two men and two women. Crewl was glad to have Willow Selong cast as Mrs. Rolle and James Talon playing Rolle's son. Both actors had been recommended by Elm as "hard workers," and at the first few rehearsals, Crewl thought they appeared to have real talent. Both would be on stage for the entire production. The other two actors made only brief appearances—one in Scene I, the other in Scene II. Crewl thought a play with a larger cast might have provided greater student opportunity, but she was confident in her ability to work well with a smaller number.

Rehearsals went well for two weeks. Selong and Talon had learned their lines and were beginning to develop believable, fully rounded characterizations. Even the overall rhythms of the play had begun to be established. In fact, before long Crewl began to wonder how she could keep the play growing for another six weeks, and how she would keep the actors interested in continued rehearsal.

The first signs of any difficulty appeared when Selong announced during the third week of rehearsal that because she was so good in the role she needed fewer rehearsals than the rest of the cast and would not attend the next rehearsal. Crewl talked with her, but to no avail. Thereafter, Willow appeared at rehearsal only occasionally. Sometimes she was gone for several consecutive days, and her absences were always unannounced and unexplained. Finally, Crewl told her the role would have to be recast if she missed another rehearsal. Willow promised to attend faithfully. When, one week later, on Thursday, she failed to show up for a scheduled time, Crewl recast the role.

On the following Monday, Talon told Crewl that over the weekend he had "found Jesus" and could no longer be in plays. He would have to drop out of the cast. After an hour-long conversation, Crewl convinced him to continue, though he said it would be a "low priority" activity for him. His sense of responsibility, he felt, meant he shouldn't quit something he had started.

Thereafter, Talon, like Willow before him, began missing

rehearsals. On such evenings, the production was virtually paralyzed. Crewl and the other actors frequently just waited for him to show up, hoping against hope that he was only late.

During the entire rehearsal period, Elm stayed away, letting Crewl handle the production by herself. "It will," he told her, "be good experience for you to have total responsibility for the play." Consequently, he did nothing to interfere, nor did he offer her advice, although he did help track down a suitable replacement for Willow. Crewl never actually talked with him about the production. On the few initial occasions when she solicited his advice, Elm made it clear that she should carry on alone. She and Lynn Ballow, however, who was directing *The Lottery* as the second play to be staged as part of the same bill, talked frequently, sharing problems, arranging schedules and designing scenery. She also discussed the situation with her supervising education instructor at Ellenberg, who encouraged her to proceed as best she could, even though he agreed it seemed to be an awkward and unhappy dilemma.

When the play finally opened, Crewl thought it to be an artistic disaster. Selong's replacement had little talent and had never appeared in a play before. Talon played half-heartedly, as if he wished he were somewhere else. Elm said nothing to her about the play one way or the other. After the third and final performance, however, he showed her a check he had received as payment for his "overload" of directing. He also asked if she would be willing to help in planning the next year's schedule of theatre classes and productions.

Questions

1. Analyze the problems which Crewl faced.

2. Analyze the decisions Crewl made. What other options, if any, were available to her?

CASE 4. RULES FOR DIRECTING

John Garcia walked into his classroom and faced for the first time some twenty senior theatre majors enrolled in Directing I, the introductory directing course for undergraduates. Without hesitation, he walked to the blackboard while saying, "Today I want us to make a list of all the important rules of directing."

He wrote on the board:

Rule #1: Don't Be Boring.

Rule #2: Don't Rely on What You Already Know.

Rule #3: Don't Be Unintelligent.

Then he turned to the students and said, "What other rules should be up here?"

Questions

1. Analyze the three rules that Garcia has written on the blackboard.

2. What rules would you add to this beginning list? Why?

3. Are any of these rules important? Why or why not?

CASE 5. THE DIRECTOR'S VOICE

Graduate student director Elodie Mains sat alone in her room late on a Thursday night. She had been asked to arrive in her third-year directing class at Gatlin University on Monday prepared to assess as fully as possible the individuality of her own directing—how she did it, what seemed to be of importance to her, what values she brought to the process, what skills she possessed, what weaknesses she needed to strengthen—everything, her professor had said, that might help to separate her from all the other theatre directors in the world, everything that contributed to her own "voice" in the theatre.

Having worked on the assignment for two weeks, Mains had begun to formulate several preliminary questions in her mind, the answers to which—she thought—could help define her own directing. The questions so far were these:

1. How do I work? (Quickly, slowly, carefully, with abandon, methodically, intuitively, alone, collegially—how?)

2. Do I expect actors to rehearse? (Or do I want performances all the time? Do I know the difference?)

3. What kind of contact do I maintain with actors?

4. What kind of contact do I maintain with the other collaborators? (Designers, stage manager, business manager, others?)

5. What do I demand? (Of myself, of others?)

6. What is my "style"? (Loud, quiet, energetic, dictatorial, businesslike, inspirational, gentle, rough, demanding, sympathetic—what?)

7. What's important to me about acting, about actors? What's important to me about the process of acting, about the end result?

8. How do I relate to other people? (As a leader, motivator, coordinator, manager, teacher, artist—how?)

9. Are intellectual ideas important to me?

10. Do I see the theatre as a social art?

Mains knew that other questions would emerge as she continued to think about it. And she knew her answers needed to be ready by Monday.

Questions

1. What other questions would you add to Mains' beginning
   list?

2. How do you, as a director, answer these questions for
   yourself at the moment? What is your "voice"?

3. What are the most important things in determining a
   director's "voice"?

Chapter II The Director: Pre-Production

CASE 6. CONFRONTING THE SCRIPT: *REHEARSAL*

Robert Lyle was to direct Benjamin Bradford's *Rehearsal* as a fully realized second season production on the Short Street Theatre's intimate, experimental stage. He had read the script three times, and he liked it. Its combination of naive innocence and adolescent leer, he thought, would appeal to those Short Street audience members who ventured away from the regional theatre's mainstage productions to see its experimental series.

In just three days he was to meet with the Short Street design staff for an initial design conference. One week later he would have auditions and go into rehearsal. The time had come for serious consideration of the play.

Questions

1. What problems will Lyle face as he approaches the direction of *Rehearsal?* How should he solve those problems?

2. What production elements will be necessary to translate *Rehearsal* into a "fully realized" production?

3. As advisor to Mr. Bradford, who will be present during rehearsals, what initial suggestion should Lyle make for revising or reworking the script?

4. How should Lyle describe the play for the design staff?

CASE 6. APPENDIX

REHEARSAL
by Benjamin Bradford

The play takes place in Clifton Mattingly's apartment, an unfurnished converted flat in the far reaches of the East Village. Only the living room, if one could call it that, can be seen or suggested. There is no furniture at all. After a moment Clifton enters. He is twenty-two, painfully shy. He walks about anxiously for a moment, then girding his shoulders, makes a ringing noise and mimes opening the door.

CLIFTON: *(Enthusiastically)* Hello. How are you? Have any trouble finding the place? *(A beat)* It's easy when you follow instructions. Not the best part of town, I guess, but it's good enough for me. Here, let me have your coat. *(Mimes taking a coat from his imaginary visitor)* Very nice coat. I like the color. *(A beat)* Is it blue? *(Again a slight pause)* Looks blue under the light. Actually, I don't have very good color sense. Can't tell blue from green, and sometimes red. I guess I don't pay enough attention. *(Slight laugh)* When I was in kindergarten I'd as well draw an elephant yellow as gray or whatever. *(Faltering)* You know. *(Mimes hanging up the coat)* Do you mind if I hang it here? *(Small laugh)* It's perfectly safe ... I'd do the sky red and the grass orange. I failed kindergarten art, and that's really failing. Did you have a good day? *(A moment)* Oh, the usual things. You know how it is in a hardware store ... busy sometimes, not so busy at others. I guess you're not too interested in that. *(Gently)* Did you have a nice day? Oh, I asked you that. You did, you said you did. It's very nice of you to come all the way down here ... in the rain. I wouldn't have asked you if I'd known it was going to rain. If I didn't want you

39

to come, I wouldn't have asked . . . You know.
(Suddenly) I guess you want to sit down.
(Crossing left) I'll get you a chair. *(He exits left
but continues to speak)* I keep the chairs in the
kitchen. Don't keep much out there. Well, the
truth is, I don't have much. You know. *(He
returns carrying a folded metal chair)* It's a
folding chair . . . *(Quickly)* But it's perfectly
safe . . . and comfortable. I think it's guaranteed to support three hundred pounds. *(Em-
barrassed laugh)* Of course, I don't think you
weight three hundred pounds . . . or anywhere
near it. I mean . . . if I did, I wouldn't have
asked you at all. I keep trim by climbing all
those stairs. Very good exercise, you know. I
go up and down them all the time. When I
moved in here two and a half months ago, I
could barely get up the first three flights
without stopping for breath, but . . . now I
don't have any trouble at all . . . just breeze up
and down like I was on the street floor. *(A
beat)* You're out of breath, I should have
noticed. *(Opening the chair)* Here, I'll fix the
chair for you. You just sit down and be
comfortable. Well, it's not as comfortable as
some, but it's more comfortable than the
floor. *(A laugh)* It's not as far down as the
floor. You know what I mean. Your color's
getting better all the time. *(Quickly)* You want
a drink, don't you? I asked you for a drink and
you want it. You see, I'm not really used to
having company. I hardly know anyone, and
when you don't know anyone, you don't have
much company. I hope you like vodka. *(A
pause)* It's all I have. Wait a minute, I have a
small bottle of red wine . . . it's sort of sour. *(A
smile)* You like red wine? But you'd rather
have vodka? Wonderful. I got some quinine
water. I hope you like quinine water. Do you
think it's too cold? Well, I mean, it's a drink

for summer, and now it's winter, and well, I'm not used to company. *(A brief pause)* Especially when they are so pretty. *(Quickly)* I'm not making fun. I think you are pretty. I like a girl that's filled out. *(A small leer)* Especially in the right places. I'm going to get some furniture up here as soon as I can or I'll find another place. I'd rather live uptown, you know, by the museum, but I just took the first place I looked at. I guess it's not too bad. *(A beat)* It's not too good either. When I have time to look around, I'll find another place. And I'll want you to come there too. I have another chair. It's in the kitchen too. You just sit there and be comfortable and I'll be right back. *(He exits left and continues to speak)* Can you hear me out there? Sound carries nicely in here . . . these thin walls. I bet you were busy today, being Friday. I didn't come in for lunch because I took a pimento cheese sandwich . . . and an apple. The pimento cheese was getting old and if I didn't eat it today, I'd just have to throw it out. And I knew I'd see you tonight anyway. I plan to be in Monday . . . same table. *(He enters with one vodka)* I had the ice and everything ready to go. I was really prepared for . . . you know. Say, you've got nice legs. I never noticed in the restaurant. You've got on a shorter skirt. Knees are nice too. You still have your baby dimples *(A beat)* I'm twenty-two. That's not so young. I've lived a long time. Twenty-two years is a long time any way you look at it. *(A slight laugh)* You don't look as if you could possibly be that old. You're not much over thirty, are you? Why should I care? *(He finishes the drink)* Well, age is relative, very relative. I meant to bring my own chair in here. I'll be right back. *(He finishes the drink)* You lean back and wait a minute, please. *(He exits and quickly returns with another chair and*

another drink) See, I have two just alike.
They're a matched set. *(A beat)* I went to
college because I didn't have anything better
to do for four years. I didn't learn a thing I
didn't know already. *(A slight pause)* You
drink very fast. *(He is drinking the second
vodka)* I could have taught school. I have a
teacher's certificate. But if you want to know
the truth, I think I'd be scared of children. *(A
laugh)* And I wanted a little excitement in the
big city first. You know. Do you think the big
city is exciting? *(A beat)* I guess it wouldn't be
to you. You have nice knees, do you mind if I
. . . ? *(Quickly)* I guess you want to finish your
drink. Do you always drink so fast? Of course,
you're thirsty after all those stairs. Now, here
you are, and here I am. Do you like it here?
Are you comfortable? I don't mind if you take
off your shoes. Wow, I believe in being
comfortable. I'll loosen my tie. *(He does)* Wow,
that's better, isn't it? I bet you never thought
you'd be up here in my apartment, drinking
vodka, with your shoes off. I bet you didn't
think that a week ago, when I walked in your
place and ordered a bowl of vegetable soup.
That was doggone good soup. You know I'm
terribly attracted to your knees. *(A beat)*
You're welcome. *(Pulling the chairs very close
together)* You feel warm. *(A pause)* Are you
warm? Must be the drink. I'm a little warm
too, even with my collar unbuttoned. *(He
unbuttons all the shirt buttons)* There, I'm not
hirsute. *(A laugh)* That means hairy. I'm not
very hairy. Of course I have hair some places
. . . but not on my chest. One or two maybe.
You want another drink? Wow, you drink
faster than any girl I ever saw. *(He rises)* Oh
sure. I've known lots of girls. Not at college, it
was a boys' school. But I went out on
weekends . . . when I wasn't studying. *(Pause)*

Yeah, it was pretty sexy being in college. I'll get you another drink. *(He finishes the drink and chokes on it)* Excuse me. You know, when you said you'd like to know me better, I was really amazed. Not a lot of people want to know me better. I'm really very shy. I don't seem to be, I know, but I am . . . and quiet, very quiet. *(Boyishly)* You hair looks clean. You must have washed it. Feels good, too. You don't mind, do you? The way the light shines on it, I could tell it was clean. *(Suddenly)* You want another drink . . . already? Sure, if you want one. *(He exists and returns with another drink)* I bet you're feeling very warm now . . . all over. I know I am. My lower lip feels numb when I drink too much. *(He drinks)* Say, I just bought a pint of vodka. I could go out and get some more. *(A pause)* Those stairs . . . I'm feeling pretty good. *(A pause)* I thought you were. I could tell. Wow, why don't we just let our hair down? You know what I mean. *(He mimes handing her the drink and drinks it himself)* God no. I'm not trying to get you drunk. *(A beat)* Or me either. I guess I could do most anything I want with you. *(Quickly)* That's not what I meant. I'd like doing things to you. *(Suddenly)* No, that's not what I meant. I mean, I'm glad you're here. *(He is getting a little high)* Yeah, they called me the quiet one. Can you believe that? I've been talking like a breeze to you. I guess you have to meet the right person to talk to. Yeah, I knew I'd come here and meet someone . . . that liked me. Yeah, I guess my leg is hot too. *(Quickly)* I'll get a better job when I have time to look for one. I'm just getting my bearings now. *(A moment)* I could always go back home, I suppose I don't much want to. Talking to my mother is like talking to nobody. It's more listening that talking anyway. *(A pause)* It's

next door . . . really part of the kitchen. That's
why the kitchen is so small. They put the
bathroom in half of it. *(Rising)* Just pull the
chain when you're through. Don't worry
about the noise, I'll hum or something. And
don't worry about the door either, I won't
come in there. I'm not that kind. I guess they
just didn't think a door was necessary. *(Sing-
ing)* "Roses are blooming in Picardy La de da,
la de da, la de da. Roses are blooming in
Picardy." *(He completes the verse whistling)*
There you are. Didn't take long at all. Yeah, it
does sound like a waterfall. Say, you know
what it really sounds like? We had a cyclone in
Georgia when I was growing up. That's exactly
the way it sounded. Boy, I won't forget that
noise. Didn't touch our house at all, but blew
two houses across the street completely away.
(He sits) I don't know where they went.
Somewhere, I guess. First thing you know,
more houses were put up, and before I could
remember how it looked before . . . I'd
forgotten *(Seriously)* The bedroom is through
the kitchen. Nicest room I've got. I brought
the chest all the way up here by myself. I'm
going to paint it when I find the time. *(A
pause)* Probably blue. Well, I don't really have
a bed yet. I don't even know how I'll get it up
the stairs. You saw how narrow the turns are.
The army cot folds up. I can take it when I
leave. *(Very close to her)* It's narrow and it's
hard, but you get used to it. Why, I've been
sleeping on it over two months, since I moved
out of the YMCA. *(A pause)* Wow, I sure
didn't think I looked that young. I guess I
ought to grow a beard or something. *(Laughs)*
As slow as it grows it'd take five or six years
then I wouldn't need to look older. *(Earnestly)*
I shave at least twice a week. If you're all that
hot, you could take off your dress. I sit around

here with nothing on most of the time. Sure, it'd be fine with me. *(A beat)* If I'd known you like to drink that much, I'd have bought a bigger bottle. Say, how'd you like the red wine? What's it matter, alcohol is alcohol. *(He exits and continues to speak)* Wait a minute. Just hang your dress on the nail by your coat. I usually put my jacket there when I come in. *(Offstage)* If you want to take something else off, feel free. I just want you to be comfortable, really comfortable. *(He returns with a glass of wine)* I thought we could share this . . . make it a loving cup. You know, you take a drink and I'll take a drink. *(He drinks)* You've got the biggest breasts I've every seen. . . . or imagined. No honest, I think they're horribly attractive. Fascinating really. *(Sitting)* Do you mind? *(Drinking)* I hope . . . well, I hope you won't think I'm too skinny. Never have been able to gain weight. Well, if you are too fat, I'm too thin. Doesn't make any difference when two people are . . . You know. *(Taking off his shirt)* I could put a towel on the chair if you're really cold. I mean, I don't want you to be cold. Here, just put my shirt on the seat. *(He put his shirt on the other chair)* Better? *(A beat)* Too much light out here. I'll take off my pants in the bedroom. *(Laughing)* Wow. No, I mean . . . if you don't think you'd fit on a cot, I could bring a blanket in here. Yeah, the floor is full of splinters. I learned that the first week I was here. Boy, I wouldn't walk on that floor without shoes for anything. *(Earnestly)* When I get up and go to the bathroom, I always put on my shoes. I have a thick blanket. A birthday present from my mother. She was scared I'd freeze up here. *(A beat)* I guess I'm not warm all the time, but I haven't frozen. *(Laughing)* Well, you can see that. *(Seriously)* Why don't you look at the

cot . . . ? You can make up your mind then.
(Rising) Now? *(A beat)* Yeah, I'm ready if you
are. Wow. I'd be happy to kiss you. *(A long
pause)* I've never been kissed like that. I didn't
know people did. Aren't you afraid of germs
and colds and things? *(A beat)* No, I'm not
afraid of anything. *(Crossing left)* Sure I'm
certain. *(Softly)* Say, wait a second . . .
Afterward . . . *(A beat)* I mean . . . well, you
know . . . *(A wistful, boyish smile)* You know .
. . after . . . I hope you still like me *(He exits
quickly)*

CURTAIN

CASE 7. THE SCRIPT IN CONTEXT: WELLINGTON COLLEGE

John Durn, Assistant Professor of Theatre at Wellington College, examined again the three short scripts that lay on his desk. He had read each of them twice. And he liked them. Even their titles seemed intriguing: *A Very Little Love Story, Balloons* and *The Mannequin*. (These plays can be found in Appendices I, II and III of this case.) He had been invited to direct the plays during the annual Festival of Exploration, a semester-long celebration to be sponsored by the college chapel. Now he needed to respond to that invitation at a breakfast meeting the next morning with Robert Kardin, the college pastor.

Background

Wellington College, a small (600 students), four-year liberal arts college supported by the Lutheran Church in America, enjoyed a reputation for academic excellence, invigorating campus environment and outstanding arts programs. Each spring these three traits were highlighted by the Festival of Exploration—an occasion during which Wellington's exceptionally bright students and highly talented faculty members explored together issues of common concern. The Festival, begun ten years earlier, had developed a large and enthusiastic audience drawn from both on and off campus, and it had become strong primarily because of Wellington's strong academic and artistic programs in the arts. The Department of Theatre, for example, employed seven full-time faculty members and produced thirty to forty different plays each year with a large core of interested and talented students.

The invitation

Dr. Durn had been at Wellington for two years and was the newest of theatre faculty members. Consequently, he felt honored to receive the following letter one morning from Pastor Kardin.

47

Dear Dr. Durn:

Once again, it is my intention in the spring term to utilize the daily chapel period at least twice each week for a Festival of Exploration. For the sake of students, faculty, staff and the many interested townspeople of Wellington, it seems good that the college chapel provide both time and place for sharing, across any discipline lines, the most interesting developments and the most important concerns of mankind.

It is by no means intended that this period be used for explicit witness to religious faith. On the contrary, it is enough if the college chapel hereby expresses its concern for the major areas of life and thought. Consequently, there will be no liturgical elements on Festival days—simply a performance or event of one half hour's duration. The time available, of course, extends from 11:30 until noon. As in the past, the Festival will include contemporary music, theatre, art, literature, film and dance, together with several addresses by currently outstanding persons from both on and off campus.

Therefore, I am writing you—as a director in the University Theatre—to make a presentation early in the term, and I am hoping you will be willing to direct one or more short plays for that presentation. To that end, I wonder if you have seen the three scripts enclosed here. They could, it seems to me, be staged within the time period. Do you think they are appropriate for the Festival?

Funds are available, of course, to defray the cost of production and to provide an honorarium to you for your work. We would also provide an honorarium to each of your cast members.

Please let me know at your earliest convenience if you will accept this invitation in order that appropriate publicity may be given to the entire series. Thank you very much.

Sincerely,

Robert Kardin

P.S. We will gladly provide alternative dates later in the term if that would be more suitable. And I am certainly open to your choosing another play or plays, should you find these particular scripts inappropriate or unacceptable.

Questions

1. What is each of these three plays about? Are they appropriate for the Festival of Exploration?

2. What physical elements are needed for the production of these plays?

3. What suggestions would you make to Dr. Durn concerning the plays and their production for the Festival of Exploration?

CASE 7. APPENDIX I

BALLOONS
by Benjamin Bradford

The set consists of two straight chairs, nothing more. At rise, there are two characters on stage: LOOMIS, a young man in coat and tie, and HARDING, slightly older, dressed in a blue collar uniform. Each is seated and holds a balloon. LOOMIS has a blue balloon, HARDING a red balloon. After each speech each man further inflates his balloon.

HARDING: *(A beat)* I really wanted the blue one.

LOOMIS: But I was given the blue one. *(Inflates)* See. Blue!

HARDING: It's the one I wanted. I didn't want the red one. *(A beat)* But it was the one I was given. They always give me the one I don't want.

LOOMIS: Do you know what you want?

HARDING: I sure as hell do. I want the blue one.

LOOMIS: Well . . . what we are allotted, we must keep. That's the way it is . . . the way it's been . . . the way it's going to be.

HARDING: Don't be so sure.

LOOMIS: You haven't looked at history.

HARDING: Sure I did. Back in high school.

LOOMIS: Inadequate.

HARDING: How can you say that?

LOOMIS: High school is a beginning. Look at you, for you it was an ending. *(Quickly)* I'm a college graduate. That's how I can say that. A college graduate can say anything. *(A beat)* It's called credibility. You wouldn't understand credibility.

HARDING: I understand . . . I'm a human . . . with rights. I have as much right to a blue balloon as you. I don't give a good damn about you being a college graduate. That's just another rich piece of paper. Rich. *(A beat)* You want to know the truth? I never met a college graduate who had a lick of sense. Common sense. Who you think gets the work done around here? Isn't the hell you. You sit on your ass in a tie . . .

LOOMIS: I don't sit on my ass in a tie. *(A superior smile)* You think you can do what I do?

HARDING: Sure. I can do nothing about as well as the next guy. *(Coldly)* But I can also get the work done. I can produce. *(Holds out his hands, keeping the balloon between his teeth)* With these. These are hands.

LOOMIS: *(Looking down)* I know what hands are.

HARDING: You just don't know what they're for. *(LOOMIS holds out his hands, keeping his balloon between his teeth)* Say, your fingernails are polished.

LOOMIS: And yours are dirty.

HARDING: *(Triumphantly)* Because I work with them. *(HARDING rises and crosses behind LOOMIS)*

LOOMIS: *(Looking forward)* Where're you going?

HARDING: *(Off handedly)* I'm going to work. *(He quickly pricks LOOMIS'S balloon with a pin, the explosion knocks LOOMIS to the floor)*

LOOMIS: Hey, you can't do that!

HARDING: *(A smile)* Can't I? *(As he exits)* Now who's got the blue one?

CURTAIN

Note: *Balloons, The Mannequin* and *A Very Little Love Story,* by Benjamin Bradford. Reprinted by permission of Benjamin Bradford. Caution: Professionals and amateurs are hereby warned that *Balloons, The Mannequin* and *A Very Little Love Story,* being fully protected under the copyright laws of the United States of America, the British Commonwealth, including The Dominion of Canada, and all other countries of the International Copyright Union and the Universal Copyright Convention, are subject to royalty. All rights, including professional, amateur, motion picture, recitation, lecturing, public hearing, radio and television broadcasting, and the rights of translation into foreign language, are strictly reserved. Particular emphasis is laid on the questions of readings, permission for which must be secured in writing from the author. All inquiries concerning rights should be addressed to the author, 122 Hilldale Lane, Paducah, KY 42001.

CASE 7. APPENDIX II

A VERY LITTLE LOVE STORY
by Benjamin Bradford

A young couple, NITA and DUANE are sitting on a small couch watching television . . . which is the audience. There is a small table next to DUANE on the couch. There is a large plastic bowl of popcorn on this table.

NITA: *(Her attention is never taken from the TV screen)*
          Oh, my God.

DUANE: What, Nita?

NITA: It's here.

DUANE: What's here?

NITA: You know.

DUANE: I don't know.

NITA: *(Takes in a breath)* It's where she finds out.

DUANE: What does she find out?

NITA: That she has . . . oh, I can't say it.

DUANE: Yeah, where she learns she has . . .

NITA: *(Dramatically)* Don't say it!

DUANE: I won't . . .

NITA: It's where she finds out that she has leukemia
          . . . that she's not long for this world. What
          happens next?

DUANE: You've seen the silly thing fifteen times. You
          know what happens next.

NITA: No, I don't. I block it out of my mind because
             I can't stand it. It simply hurts too much.
             Hurts *me* too much, so I just block it out, and
             I don't remember a thing until I see it again.
             (A beat) Fifteen times?

DUANE: At least. You've seen it with me fifteen times,
             and you've done it on your own a couple of
             times . . . maybe more.

NITA: Oh, I don't remember anything. *(DUANE
             takes a large handful of popcorn)*

DUANE: Well, I can tell you.

NITA: *(Quickly)* No, let me suffer alone. *(DUANE
             fills his mouth with popcorn and begins to chew
             it)*

NITA: And that's our song they're playing. I suppose
             that's why this all means so much to me.
             Duane. They're playing our song. Do you
             remember the very first time we saw it?

DUANE: *(His mouth full)* Mmmmmmmmmmmmmm.

NITA: And how wonderful it was to fall in love . . .
             the way we did. Every time I hear our song I
             think about leukemia. And I think about how
             it was with you and me and we were so happy
             . . . but they were so happy too when they
             finally got together and just look what hap-
             pened. It's just too sad, I can't bear to watch it.
             (A beat) But I will. I will see it to the end.
             *(DUANE begins to noiselessly choke on the
             popcorn, he puts his hands to his throat, his eyes
             bulge)*

NITA: I sometimes think if you should get leukemia,
             I couldn't stand it. I could just die when I

think about it. *(A beat as DUANE continues to choke)* You know I never think about me getting leukemia, just you. *(DUANE falls from the couch, dead)* Isn't that funny? I guess that is real love.

BLACKOUT

CASE 7. APPENDIX III

THE MANNEQUIN
by Benjamin Bradford

At rise a very fashionably dressed mannequin is standing with her back to the audience. JIM, a young man, is sitting in a nearby chair.

JIM: *(As if continuing an argument)* Of course I think you're the best dressed woman I know. *(A beat)* With the best figure. And I love you because you don't talk all the time . . . like most women. You don't gossip. You've got good habits. What more do you want me to say? *(A beat)* You want to dance? *(A beat)* Oh, I'm a very good dancer. Very, very good. If you don't want to dance, you don't have to. Okay, I'm tired too. *(A beat)* And there's no music. Well, I have music . . . if there's anything I have, it's music, and if there's anything I do well, it's turning on the stereo. *(A beat)* Do you want music? *(A beat)* You don't want music. Anybody looks as good as you ought to want to go out dancing. *(A knock on the door)* Who's that? *(He rises)* You've got another boyfriend, don't you? You don't think I'm good enough for you. *(Stronger)* You don't give me a chance. I can talk to a girl as well as the next guy, maybe better. *(Another knock on the door)* Well, why don't you answer it? I'm not going to make a scene, a jealous scene. I'm not that kind. *(Loudly in the mannequin's ear)* I'll answer it. *(A few steps away, he turns back to her)* If you think I'm jealous, you're crazy. *(JIM opens the door, HARRY enters)*

HARRY: *(A pause)* Jim?

JIM: Yeah, I'm Jim. *(Indicates the mannequin)* She's been waiting for you.

HARRY: *(Puzzled)* Who?

JIM: *(Pointing to the mannequin)* Her.

HARRY: *(Crossing to the mannequin)* This one?

JIM: *(Strongly)* She's mine.

HARRY: *(Turning to him)* You all right, Jim?

JIM: I was . . . until you came in here. You think you can dance better than me, don't you?

HARRY: I don't think I ever thought about it.

JIM: She called you didn't she?

HARRY: Well . . . no.

JIM: Hell she didn't. *(A beat)* See that outfit?

HARRY: *(A pause)* Yeah, it's nice.

JIM: I bought it for her. Very expensive. *(A look)* What'd you promise her?

HARRY: *(Stronger)* I don't even know her. You're kidding me, aren't you, Jim? Playing a game?

JIM: Don't think you can come in here . . . and take her away from me without a fight. You may look better than I look and you may have a better personality. I can still fight for the girl I love.

HARRY: *(Sitting)* Yeah, you're playing a game. She's a big doll. You're playing with dolls.

JIM: But I've got sex appeal. She won't go out with you, I don't care what you buy her . . . what you promise her, she won't go.

HARRY: *(Rising)* Like the rest of them? Like all the
            girls we've known, Jim. You want to bet?

JIM: *(Almost triumphant)* Yeah, I'll bet you any-
            thing. She won't go out with you. *(HARRY
            stares at JIM for a moment and crosses to the
            mannequin)*

HARRY: *(To the mannequin)* Hey, Doll . . .

JIM: She won't go . . .

HARRY: *(Seductively)* Hey . . . Doll. *(A beat)* This is
            Harry.

JIM: You see . . . she's staying with me.

HARRY: *(Picks up the mannequin)* We'll have dinner
            first. I know just the right place for a girl like
            you . . . and afterwards . . . we'll let nature take
            its course. *(He walks out with the mannequin)*
            See you later, Jim.

JIM: *(Sinking into the chair)* God damned women
            . . . they're all alike.

BLACKOUT

CASE 8. THE PHYSICAL ENVIRONMENT: *THE BIRDS*

James A. Peddleton, director of the Hofstrel Theatre, was trying to decide how to stage Aristophanes' *The Birds.* Scheduled to open in early March as the fifth play of the Hofstrel 1982–83 season of plays, the classic comedy had been planned as a proscenium production in Hofstrel's regular 400-seat theatre. As Peddleton studied the play, however, he became convinced that it would work better in a smaller, more intimate, non-frontal space. In fact, the more he prepared, the more he leaned toward a semi-environmental production with both the audience and the playing space arranged on the Hofstrel stage itself. Yet he knew that such a production would reduce seating capacity drastically. He also thought the whole idea might be construed as too experimental for Hofstrel's regular season patrons.

His enthusiasm mixed with practical reservations, Peddleton presented the idea to Hofstrel's Board of Directors at its regularly scheduled monthly meeting in November. Board members had responded, as he had known they would, by confirming his role as Artistic Director and by encouraging him to consider not only *The Birds* as he decided, but also Hofstrel's total season and image. After discussing briefly the artistic and economic impact of changing *The Birds,* the Board had asked Peddleton to explore the idea further and to make a final recommendation at its scheduled meeting in December.

Less than a week now remained before the December meeting. Peddleton knew that his recommendation should be one that both he and the Board could support. Either he could leave *The Birds* as it had been originally planned, or he could change it to fit more precisely his developing production concept.

Background

The idea for an environmental production of *The Birds* came to Peddleton early in his preparation process. After reading the play only a few times, he began to think that an ancient

59

play—one presented to its audience as a "classic"—might seem less remote and more approachable if presented in a very contemporary mode. He envisioned an audience close to the action, in a theatre setting that provided the possibility for multiple focus, simultaneous staging and an informal atmosphere—all of which seemed to Peddleton very indicative of Greek comedy. As this thinking progressed, he began to see a specific playing space, one that presented greater possibilities for action than a normal proscenium stage might offer. He had even drawn a rough ground plan of the space, more to establish an idea than to design a setting, but one that represented the kind of actor/audience relationship he envisioned. (This rough ground plan is reproduced in Appendix I of this case.) He imagined the audience divided into several distinct pockets, and a stage divided into several playing areas connected by ramps and crosswalks.

Such an idea, Peddleton realized, was not new, but the discovery of it was new for him, and he realized it might seem even radical to Hofstrel's regular subscription audience. After all, every Hofstrel production for more than fifteen years had been presented on a proscenium stage, and its audience had been conditioned to a very traditional kind of theatre. Yet the more he thought, the more committed to the idea he became.

Hofstrel theatre

A long-established community theatre in a large, metropolitan Southern city. Hofstrel employed a year-round professional staff that included Peddleton, a scenic and lighting designer, a costumer, three persons in public relations and audience development, and a business manager. Each of these seven persons, plus five community volunteers, served on Hofstrel's Board of Directors. The five non-employees, elected on a rotating basis by the large Hofstrel membership, served as an executive committee for the theatre, responsible for the development of ongoing policy and for the hiring and firing of theatre employees.

The 1982–83 season of plays followed a pattern established eight years earlier when the theatre had moved into its own newly constructed building. Each year the season opened in November with a comedy and closed in March with a classic. During December, January and February, it presented primarily modern plays chosen for wide audience appeal. For 1982–83, the season included *You Can't Take It with You, Life with Father, The Glass Menagerie, A Man for All Seasons* and *The Birds.* Each production played five performances a week for four weeks. Rehearsals for each play began as soon as the production which preceded it opened.

James Peddleton had been employed by the theatre for five seasons and he directed each of the regular productions. He also directed the two special children's plays that toured to public schools in a tri-state area throughout April and May of each year. (Heavily supported by business, foundation and state money, the school tour employed a small company of professional actors and technicians hired by Hofstrel for three months each spring.) Peddleton also directed two of the four plays staged by Hofstrel during its summer season in June and July. The theatre was dark in August, while the staff was on vacation, and in September and October, when preparation for the winter season began.

While the Hofstrel Board of Directors maintained ultimate artistic and fiscal authority over the theatre's operations, it had delegated artistic decision-making to the professional staff director. Peddleton had established a good working relationship with all Board members, especially the non-theatre employees. Never had he made artistic decisions single-handedly or without full consultation with everyone concerned. Consequently, when he suggested the possibility of staging *The Birds* in a non-proscenium manner, the Board had listened eagerly. It had also agreed to delay consideration of the matter until its December meeting, before which time concerned members could write to Peddleton expressing their views on the matter. This was a standard Hofstrel procedure when major decisions had to be recommended.

Once Peddleton had received all the written statements (which are reproduced in Appendix II of this case), he realized his decision, whatever it might be, would not meet with unanimous approval. He also realized that not everyone on the Board had responded.

Questions

1. What factors should Peddleton consider as he chooses a production space for *The Birds?* Which are most important?

2. Which alternative should Peddleton choose?

3. Prepare a rationale supporting that choice for Peddleton to present at the December Board meeting.

Ground Plan

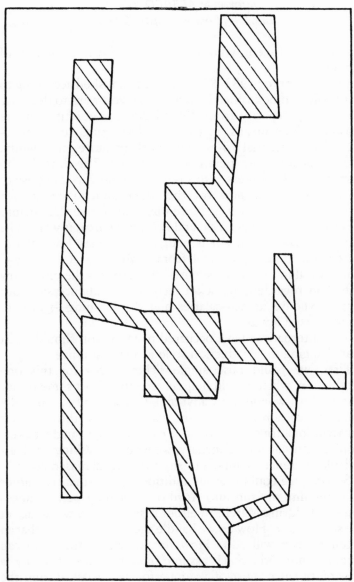

Lined areas are acting space; unlined areas are audience space.

CASE 8. APPENDIX II

Statement of ALFRED JONES,
Business Manager, Hofstrel Theatre

Jim, the way I see it, your decision boils down to a matter of money.

Our budget for 1982–83 has been established according to our projected box-office income. Now you want to decrease our seating capacity from 400 to 200 for one-fifth of the season—which means, in essence, decreasing our total income by a potential 10 percent. Perhaps more importantly, you would decrease potential income for *The Birds* by 50 percent. My best guess at this point suggests if you choose to do *The Birds* in this new way, then the production budget for it would need to be cut by more than half. We're already into *You Can't Take It with You,* and *Life with Father* is well on its way. *The Glass Menagerie* is budgeted at a very low level to start with. Unless you steal from *A Man for All Seasons*— which wouldn't seem to be wise—*The Birds* is the only show left. And regardless of ticket income or audience size, our major expense items—salaries and the building—will continue at fixed levels.

Two alternatives have occurred to me if you should insist that changing the production style is our best move.

First, we could raise single ticket prices for this one production, which would help us recoup at least some of our losses. But I wonder how advisable that would be, especially since we've already sold so many tickets through our subscription drive. In essence, even though single tickets won't go on sale until February, we would be asking our least reliable audience members to support our increased costs.

Second, we could present additional performances, either by extending the run into April or by adding performances somehow during March. In either case, what do we do about the school tour? How do we handle the increased costs that an extended run will add? How do you get actors who can commit more time? (I assume matinees aren't really a possibility since most of your performers work during the day.)

In short, we've got a money problem. I think we'd better just do *The Birds* as originally planned. Anything else would seem to lead directly to financial difficulty.

Statement from SUZANNE WOLFE,
Scenic and Lighting Designer, Hofstrel Theatre

My God! This is the first really exciting idea I've heard since coming to Hofstrel in 1980. It's really a chance to do something different, and your beginning ideas seem to bring the play to new life. As a designer, I'd love it. I also think your rough sketch idea has all kinds of possibilities and would be a great place for us to start working together on a finished design.

But!

And it's a big one!

Where will we get time to build this "monster" between when *Man for All Seasons* closes and *The Birds* opens? I mean, we have to build a stage and an auditorium. Then we have to build a set to go on it. In the five days we now have as turn-around time? Even if we can find the time, where do we find the people? You know the number of scene shop volunteers is limited. I wonder if we could encourage more to show up. What do you think?

Lighting, of course, presents some additional problems. I think we could do it, but it will mean rehanging everything and running cables everywhere—which means we need even more people in the same five days.

One thing to think about would be renting platforms or something for the audience. This might save us some time even though it would place some limitations on the overall design.

Statement of JOHN W. MCDONALD,
President, Hofstrel Theatre

Dear Mr. Peddleton:

We've had a good relationship since I became President last year, so I know I can speak frankly.

I was silent at our November meeting when you first

suggested producing *The Birds* in some new and different way, but we've already announced a plan for the season and now we should stick to it. People just don't make changes like this in the middle of the year. It's bad public relations. Even if your idea for *The Birds* is a good one (and I'm not quite willing to grant that it is), we just can't do it now. It would be too disruptive all the way around. I would hate to lose what we've all spent so long building up. I would also hate to see your outstanding leadership diminished and tarnished in the eyes of the Executive Committee.

Thank goodness, you've always been a reasonable person. I'm sure you'll continue to be reasonable as you prepare for our December meeting.

Statement from BEVERLY LEVITTS,
Public Relations, Audience Development, Hofstrel Theatre

I'll be direct. Your idea for *The Birds* presents some real problems.

First, we've already sold tickets for the show. Reserved seats! How upset, if at all, will those audience people be if we tell them there has been a change of plans and they need to move from their comfortable, upholstered seats (which some of them have been sitting in for many years) to a kind of "pioneering," temporary arrangement up on the stage? Folding chairs? Stools? What? Also, it will cost us some money and time to contact these people ahead of time.

Second, I assume we'd have to have a whole new set of tickets printed.

Third, as you well know, we are building a larger and larger audience. Our average attendance last year was 325 people per performance. That's about an 80 percent capacity figure. On weekends we played to about 98 percent consistently. This year we've sold (as of 11/7/82) about 125 season tickets for each available night. If our past record continues, and if you reduce the number of seats for *The Birds* to 200 . . . Well, you can see the problem. I'm not worried about any loss of income; no doubt Alfred has talked to you about whether or not that would make a difference. I'm worried about turning away so many people. This would be especially hard if the production turns out to be a hit. I also worry a little about any audience members we might lose by being so adventuresome or by making this change so late.

Statement from SHARON BREWSTER,
Advertising and Publicity, Hofstrel Theatre

I can sell it, Jim, with no problems. In fact, given our attendance figures from last year, our current advance sale, and a maximum audience size of only 200, I can virtually guarantee you sold-out houses for every performance. If we added just three performances each (I think we could easily do two shows each on Friday and Saturday nights—I've been arguing that for two years) then we would end up with only twenty-five fewer available seats each week than we usually sell. Any loss of income would be negligible, as would any increase in costs. I don't know whether or not you can spring actors free for additional performances, but that's another problem. Anyone who auditioned would know about the schedule before getting involved, and with the large core of eager actors you've built up, it shouldn't make any difference. Should it?

The real challenge, from my point of view, will be announcing the change so that our audience will feel excited about it. We've never done anything like this before, which means we'll have to guess how our fairly traditional and conservative audience might respond. It is a comedy, and that should help. But at least part of our audience, as you know, will object if you mess around with a classic this way.

I really think it's a good idea. If it doesn't work out for *The Birds,* perhaps we can plan something for next year—or for the summer.

Also—Beverly talked to me yesterday about her season subscription people, the ones who already have reserved-seat tickets. She's especially worried about people like Mrs. Wilkes and Dr. and Mrs. Henderville—those who always insist on the same seats year after year and who support the theatre fairly heavily through their contributions. I think, however, that we can move them without too much difficulty—as long as we have enough lead time. I can help her make them feel good about the change. It would be a real PR challenge—a chance to change attitudes—or at least a chance to try.

Statement from ELMER G. FITZGERALD,
Secretary, Hofstrel Theatre Executive Committee

TO: James Peddleton
FROM: Elmer "Hap" Fitzgerald

I'm addressing this letter to you, and I'm sending copies to the entire Board so they will all know how I feel.

For too long this theatre has been governed solely by practical considerations. We hired you as Artistic Director, and I say if you want to do *The Birds* in some experimental way, let's do it. Our job on the Board—especially for those of us elected by the membership—should be to make possible whatever you as Artistic Director think will work best.

So, you decide. Then we will support your decision in every possible way. Needless to say, I think the problems of tickets, extending the run, finding extra money, adding extra performances—I think all of these can be solved without too much difficulty if we all work together.

cc: Hofstrel Theatre Board of Directors

Statement from RUSTY GABRIEL,
Hofstrel Costumer

Jim, we've already talked, so you know that from a practical point of view whatever gets done with *The Birds* is fine with me. Either way, it will be an expensive show to costume—anytime there are that many bodies to cover the costs go up. So I would worry some if reducing the audience size would also reduce the costume budget. But at the same time, you know by now how I work: tell me how much money I have to spend and I'll do the show for that much.

At the same time, I support your idea and would like to see

the concept carried out. Not only would it be great fun, it might help our audience mature by exposing them to a new theatre idea. They need this. And we need to provide it for them. In fact, we have a real responsibility to do just that. I've worried for four years now, ever since I started here at Hofstrel that we're not challenging anybody—just providing a constant stream of escape. *The Birds* could help solve that dilemma for me.

I'm also sure that John McDonald will be absolutely opposed to the idea. But please remember that he's against anything new every time something gets suggested. As long as he doesn't have to do any of the work involved, he'll be happy.

It seems to me the only real dilemma is this: what do we do about all the people who'll want to see it who won't be able to get in?

Statement from CHARLES HARBINGER,
Member, Hofstrel Theatre Executive Committee

Like so many other citizens in this community, I have watched the Hofstrel Theatre grow and develop over the fifteen years of its existence. I even take some pride in knowing that I have helped that growth, having served two different four-year terms on the Board. I've known and worked with all four Artistic Directors during that time, including you during your first two years. Now that my third full term as a Board member is beginning, I hope to help that growth continue, and I have committed myself to continuing the strong traditions established by this organization.

Consequently, I must oppose your idea for staging *The Birds* as if it were a radical, experimental work of the 1960's. It is not. And Hofstrel is not an off-off-Broadway rendezvous for such freaky fare. *The Birds* is a classic play that deserves a production with real decorum, not a production that follows some wild-eyed scheme like you suggest.

Hofstrel has long been a traditional theatre presenting traditional plays in a traditional way. This is our greatest strength, and should continue to be so. Our large audience following and our large corps of volunteers have responded well to such a program—and we should not do anything that might prove detrimental to that support.

You may be interested to know that I have shared your idea with about twenty of my friends, all of whom are Hofstrel season subscribers. With few exceptions, these people would not like to see *The Birds* presented as you have suggested. Some, in fact, are vehement in their feelings. Many have said they would not attend the performance at all. No one has yet suggested cancelling his season ticket, but I assure you that would happen.

This may be one time, if you decide to persist, that the Board needs to assert its authority and overrule your decision as Artistic Director. Certainly I will argue that position at our December meeting.

I've often thought that theatre employees should not serve on the Board. Perhaps we should also discuss this at the December meeting.

CASE 9. CHOOSING SPACE:
FLOATING THEATRE COMPANY

"I can take any space," wrote director Peter Brook, "and call it a bare stage." Jeremy Arrowsmith read these words in *The Empty Space* and thought, "Actually, directors often have no choice about the space they must take. They are given both a theatre and a stage, then told to direct a play." Arrowsmith also knew, however, that only rarely would such a space be totally inflexible; almost always a director can make at least some choices about how best the given space might be used for a specific production. Occasionally, he knew, directors faced even greater flexibility: then, as Brook implies, they were given the opportunity to choose a particular space for a particular play.

Arrowsmith thought about the possibilities as he began planning his next production for the Floating Theatre Company, for he had been given just that opportunity: a chance to perform anywhere in the city, in a theatre or in any other space he might choose. As he thought, he began to create a series of questions concerning performance space, and he promised an answer to each question once he had chosen a play to direct.

Should there be one space, where the actors and audience mingle together in some appropriate way, or should there be two spaces, where the actors and audience are separated?

Should the space be a recognizable, formal theatre, or should it be a found or created non-theatre environment?

What should be the ideal actor/audience relationship for the play?

Should everyone in the audience see everything that happens in the performance area? If not, how much or how little should each audience member see?

Should everyone in the audience hear everything that happens in the performance area? If not, how much or how little should each audience member hear?

Should each audience member see and hear the same things as every other audience member?

Should audience members see one another?

Should the audience remain stationary throughout the

performance? Or should they move about? Should their heads need to move? Just their eyes? Not even their eyes?

Should the audience sit? On chairs? On the floor? On pillows? On bleachers?

Should audience members look up to see the play? Or down? Or both? Should they look in front? Or behind? Or all around?

Should the audience all sit together? Or should they be separated somehow? In small groups? Individually?

How many persons should be in the audience? Five? Five hundred?

How crowded or uncrowded should the audience be when they are gathered together? Should they be comfortable?

What is the audience's role in the performance? Voyeurs: watchers only? Participants: to what degree and how?

Should there be one acting space, one stage? Or should there be more than one? How many? Where?

Should the performance area be flat? Or should it be raked? Multileveled? Circular? Square?

How large or small should the performance area(s) be? Should there be any entrances or exits?

What . . . ?

The questions could go on, Arrowsmith knew, but he had begun to see the kind of possibilities that would exist. He also saw that the wisdom with which the options were selected might well determine how effective a given space could be for a particular production.

Questions

1. Analyze Arrowsmith's questions. What are the implications inherent in each of them?

2. What are some other questions about performance space that a director should consider?

Note: This brief is adapted from an article written by J. Robert Wills. Titled "Spaced Out," it appeared in *Asbestos Curtain* (April 1978).

CASE 10. PREPARING A PRODUCTION: MINTEN UNIVERSITY

Minten University had an active program of student produced and directed productions. Each year there were some one hundred performances of fifty such productions, which ranged from full-length, fully mounted plays to minimally produced one-acts performed at various times in various places. Potential student directors were asked to submit ideas for productions at any time during the year. In addition to several practical questions (title of the play, cast size, proposed dates and place of performance, etc.), each director was asked on the application for production to submit written (though brief) answers to the following questions: 1) What is this play about? 2) Describe the production you envision. 3) Why do you want to direct this play?

The applications were reviewed by a small panel of faculty and students. Approved productions were then scheduled as part of the theatre calendar.

Questions

1. Are these useful questions to ask a director? Why?

2. What other questions might also be useful for a review panel like the one at Minten? Why?

Chapter III   The Director: Casting and Rehearsals

CASE 11. PLANNING AUDITIONS: *STORY THEATRE*

Director Jerry Mode finished reading Paul Sills' *Story Theatre* one final time, then turned his thoughts to auditions for the play, scheduled now less than a week away. As an experienced director who had worked both in universities and in the professional regional theatre, he had grown increasingly unhappy with traditional audition techniques during which actors presented prepared monologues, read from the script, tried an improvisation or two, and perhaps sang a song. For one thing, he thought, such auditions asked the actors primarily for a verbal, linear, sequential presentation, while he saw the art of acting as primarily non-verbal, non-linear, and non-sequential. For another thing, he thought the usual audition often focused on performance, the end result, not on how the actor might work or on how the evolution of the end performance might emerge. In addition, he thought the usual audition procedures required the director not so much to see what was really there, but rather to guess at what wasn't there—how well an actor reading Romeo, for example, might possibly play Macbeth.

"Why shouldn't I," Mode thought, "do some things at auditions that will help me be more effective as I try to cast this play? And why shouldn't these things," he continued, "be things that relate specifically to me as a director, as well as to the play I'm about to direct?"

"What do I like in auditions?" he mused. And then he wrote the following:

1. I like auditions that enable actors to work in groups. After all, that's how a play happens. Then, among other things, I can begin to see how individual actors relate to other people and to situations.

2. I like auditions that help actors to be loose, free, not self-conscious, that let them do more than perform.

3. I like auditions that let actors do things that I want done as well as things that they want to do.

4. I like auditions that are, first of all, fun, even while they demand rigor, concentration and discipline. (Those qualities,

interestingly enough and not surprisingly, are also what I look for in rehearsals.)

5. I also like auditions that help me discover the following about each "auditionee":
   a. level of potential concentration
   b. speed of response to new ideas
   c. the flexibility and control of the instrument (voice, mind, imagination)
   d. his or her response to me, as a director, as a person
   e. my response to him or her, as an actor, as a person
   f. willingness to try new things, to meet the unexpected
   g. listening ability
   h. ability to portray character
   i. ability to transmit energy, emotion, intensity, mood
   j. willingness to be open, to rehearse

As Mode reviewed his list, he began to think specifically about auditions for *Story Theatre.*

Questions

1. What would you have actors do to accomplish what Mode likes about auditions?

2. What do you, as a director, like in auditions?

3. What would you have actors do to accomplish these ends?

CASE 12. SCHEDULING REHEARSALS:
THE WALTZ OF THE TOREADORS

The University Theatre at Walls College began producing
plays with student actors and faculty directors in 1909, but
only since 1978 had there been a fully trained theatre staff
and an undergraduate major in theatre arts. The usual pattern
of production called for open auditions followed by five
weeks of evening rehearsals which led to eighteen performances spread over a three-week period. Audience members
came primarily from the surrounding urban community, and
acting in one of UT's plays was considered to be a primary
artistic accomplishment for students. The quality of production and acting was consistently good, well received by both
critics and audience members.

Consequently, second year faculty member Robert George
felt great responsibility when selected to direct UT's final
mainstage production of the 1981–82 season, Jean Anouilh's
The Waltz of the Toreadors. A serious comedy, like much of
Anouilh's work, *The Waltz of the Toreadors* focused on the
conflict between integrity and compromise, and its fast-paced
action revolved around activity in the household of General
St. Pe. George had decided to emphasize the play's farcical
qualities, so that the more poignant moments—and especially
the phantasmagorical scene between the General and his wife
at the end of Act II—could stand more effectively in contrast
to the comic elements. His thorough pre-production work
with the script and with the various designers had brought the
production to a state of readiness almost a full week before
auditions.

As part of his preparation George had decided to give real
responsibility to three senior theatre majors who had offered
to work closely with him on the production: James Douglas
(Stage Manager), Ruth Grover (Assistant Stage Manager),
and Michael Charles (Assistant to the Director). As an initial
step in this process, he asked each of them about a week
before auditions to prepare a scheme and schedule for the
first week of rehearsal. Assured that each could do this, he

promised to use one of the schedules without change, thinking this commitment might help the three learn more from their production activity. He gave each of them a script, talked with them briefly about Anouilh's scene structure for the play (see Appendix I, this case), the characters involved (see Appendix II, this case), and gave them his own compilation of when characters were on stage throughout the play (see Appendix III, this case). He also told them of his hopes for the first week:

> We have five weeks, which is plenty long enough if time is used wisely. So the first week can proceed without any sense of time pressure. I hope we can begin the process of building an ensemble, of establishing a pattern for professional discipline, of creating a sense of efficiency. I don't want to waste time. And I don't want the actors to think they are wasting time. Within this framework there are many ways to begin.
>
> On the Sunday after auditions, I'll meet with the cast to talk and read through the script. Your schedules should start with Monday. Remember that we'll rehearse from 7 to 10 p.m. each night. It's important during the first week that we end promptly.

Douglas, Grover and Charles worked hard, drawing on their individual past experiences and their hopes for this production. Three days before auditions each presented George with the results of his or her work.

Douglas conceived a straightforward schedule that arranged rehearsals by Anouilh's scenes in the script (see Appendix IV, this case). Charles broke the play into smaller units, based primarily on exits and entrances, then arranged rehearsals with these units (see Appendix V and Appendix VI of this case). Grover approached the problem in a third and different way (see Appendix VII of this case). As George studied the three proposals he knew that each presented different problems and benefits; he knew, too, that each might accomplish vastly different purposes, and that for his cast the first week would establish patterns for succeeding weeks.

Questions

1. Analyze the three possible rehearsal schedules.

2. Which schedule should George select?

3. What other possibilities exist for scheduling a first week of rehearsal?

CASE 12. APPENDIX I

THE WALTZ OF THE TOREADORS
written by Jean Anouilh
translated by Lucienne Hill

The Scenes

The action of the play takes place in the study of General St. Pe, and in his wife's adjoining bedroom.

Act One

Scene 1:   The Study; a spring afternoon

Scene 2:   The Study; a few minutes later

Act Two

Scene 1:   The Study; a few minutes later

Scene 2:   The Bedroom; immediately following

Act Three

The Study; evening

CASE 12. APPENDIX II

THE WALTZ OF THE TOREADORS
The Cast

Mme. St. Pe

General St. Pe

Gaston, the Secretary

Sidonia

Estelle

Dr. Bonfant

First Maid

Mlle. de Ste-Euverte

Mme. Dupont Fredaine

Father Ambrose

New Maid

CASE 12. APPENDIX III

THE WALTZ OF THE TOREADORS

Act I.1 / Act I.2 / Act II.1 — Page Number

Character	5	6	7	8	9	10	11	12	13	14	15	16	17	18	19	20	21	22	23	24	25	26	27	28	29	30	31	32	33	34	35	36	37	38	39	40	41	42	43	44
Mme. St. Pe	X	X																																				X		
Gen. St. Pe			X	X	X	X	X	X	X	X	X	X	X	X	X	X	X	X	X	X	X	X	X	X	X	X	X	X	X	X	X	X	X	X	X	X	X	X	X	X
Gaston			X	X	X	X														X	X	X	X																	
Sidonia									X	X																				X	X									
Estelle									X	X																				X	X	X	X							
Dr. Bonfant							X	X						X	X	X	X	X	X	X	X	X		X	X	X	X	X												
First Maid												X								X				X																
Mme. - Euverte									X	X	X	X	X	X			X			X	X	X	X	X	X													X	X	
Mme. - Fredaine																																	X	X						
Father Ambrose																																								
New Maid																																								

Act II.2 / Act III — Page Number

Character	45	46	47	48	49	50	51	52	53	54	55	56	57	58	59	60	61	62	63	64	65	66	67	68	69	70	71	72	73
Mme. St. Pe	X	X	X	X	X	X	X	X	X	X	X																X		
Gen. St. Pe	X	X	X	X	X	X	X	X	X	X	X	X	X	X	X	X	X	X	X	X	X	X	X	X	X	X	X	X	X
Gaston																X				X	X	X	X	X	X	X	X		
Sidonia																								X	X				
Estelle																								X	X				
Dr. Bonfant													X	X	X	X				X	X	X	X	X	X	X	X	X	X
First Maid														X	X														
Mme. - Euverte												X	X	X	X	X	X	X	X	X	X	X	X	X	X				
Mme. - Fredaine																													
Father Ambrose																		X	X	X	X	X							
New Maid																												X	X

CASE 12. APPENDIX IV

THE WALTZ OF THE TOREADORS
Rehearsal Schedule: Week One
(Prepared by James Douglas)

Monday
    7:00—Block Act I

Tuesday
    7:00—Block Act II

Wednesday
    7:00—Block Act III

Thursday
    7:00—Act II, Scene 2
    8:30—Act I, Scene 2

Friday
    7:00—Act I, Scene 1
    8:30—Act II, Scene 1

Saturday
    7:00—Act III

CASE 12.   APPENDIX V

THE WALTZ OF THE TOREADORS
Rehearsal Units
(Prepared by Michael Charles)

Unit	*Pages*	*Characters*
A	5–6	GP, MP
B	7–10	GP, GA, SI, ES
C	10–11	GP, DB
D	12–17	FM, MS, GP, SI, ES, DB
E	17–25	GP, DB, (MS)
F	25–28	FM, MS, GA, GP, MP
G	29–33	GP, DB
H	33	GP, DB, GA
I	33–35	GP, GA, SI, ES, MD
J	35–37	GP, ES, SI
K	37–38	GP, MD, GA, ES, SI
L	38–43	GP, GA
M	43–44	GP, GA, MP, MD
N	44–48	GP, MP
O	48–50	GP, MP
P	50–54	GP, MP
Q	54–56	GP, MP
R	57–59	DB, GP
S	59–60	DB, GP, FM
T	60–61	GP, DB, GA, MS
U	61–64	GP, MS
V	64–67	GP, MS, GA, DB
W	67–70	GP, MS, GA, DB, FA
X	70–71	GP, MS, GA, DB, FA, SI, ES
Y	71–72	DB, GP
Z	72	GP, MP
ZZ	72–73	GP, NM

Character Key

MP = Mme. St. Pe
GP = General St. Pe
GA = Gaston, the Secretary
SI = Sidonia
ES = Estelle
DB = Dr. Bonfant

FM = First Maid
MS = Mlle. de Ste-Euverte
MD = Mme. Dupont Fredaine
FA = Father Ambrose
NM = New Maid

CASE 12. APPENDIX VI

THE WALTZ OF THE TOREADORS
Rehearsal Schedule: Week One
(Prepared by Michael Charles)

Monday	Wednesday	Friday
7:00–C	7:00–V	7:00–Q
7:30–G	7:25–W	7:15–P
8:10–R	7:45–X	7:30–N
8:35–Y	8:00–D	8:00–O
9:00–E	8:40–F	8:20–Z
9:30–ZZ	9:10–K	8:30–A
	9:30–U	8:40–ZZ
Tuesday	9:45–H	8:50–J
		9:10–K
7:00–Z	*Thursday*	9:25–I
7:20–A		9:35–X
7:40–N	7:00–I	9:50–H
8:00–O	7:30–M	
8:10–P	7:40–T	*Saturday*
8:30–Q	8:00–S	
9:00–B	8:20–D	7:00–W
9:20–J	8:50–G	7:20–V
9:35–L	9:10–C	7:45–F
	9:25–Y	8:10–T
	9:45–R	8:30–M
		8:45–B
		9:10–S
		9:20–U
		9:35–E
		9:50–L

CASE 12. APPENDIX VII

THE WALTZ OF THE TOREADORS
Rehearsal Schedule: Week One
(Prepared by Ruth Grover)

Monday

7:00 — *Company:* physical and vocal exercises, plus group acting explorations
9:00 — Work Act III around a table

Tuesday

7:00 — *Company:* physical and vocal exercises, plus theatre games
9:00 — Work Act II, Scene 2, around a table

Wednesday

7:00 — *Company:* physical and vocal exercises
8:00 — *Company:* improvisations based on actual situations in the play
9:00 — Work Act II, Scene 1, around a table

Thursday

7:00 — *Company:* physical and vocal exercises
8:00 — *Company:* improvisational character games, based on actual characters in the play
9:00 — Work Act I, Scene 2, around a table

Friday

7:00 — *Company:* physical and vocal exercises
8:00 — *Company:* individual and collective character work
9:00 — Work Act I, Scene 1, around a table

Saturday

7:00 — *Company:* physical and vocal exercises
7:30 — Work entire play around a table

CASE 13. THE FIRST REHEARSAL: A CONVERSATION

John came into the room quietly so he wouldn't interrupt the conversation taking place among members of his directing class. He heard Gail say, "No, I think the director at a first rehearsal should say nothing at all—nothing about the script, the characters, the author—nothing! I mean, it's the job of the actors to discover for themselves what is important. That's what rehearsals are for. It is not the job of the director to tell them anything at all, especially to give long, explanatory notes about just how she sees the production. That wastes time and suggests that the director is a dictator whose mind is already made up. I say, just begin. Then you can get on to the second rehearsal more quickly."

Warren disagreed.

"You're wrong, Gail," he said. "It's at this very moment, before a cast reads a script together for the first time, that a director can influence most completely how people think. That's when he can shape the production to his own concept and help the actors understand the framework for the production. He can set this particular production apart from any other production of the play. Frankly, actors are appreciative when a director tells them, up front, what he thinks."

"At the very least," John chimed in, "the director ought to say something about the set, perhaps talk about the costumes—you know, deal with practical things, so the actors don't have to ask questions about them."

Question

1. Would you tend to agree with Gail or Warren or John? What, indeed, should a director say to a cast before a first rehearsal?

CASE 14. LEARNING LINES: *AMERICAN DECIPHER*

Robert Jones cast the winter repertory production of *American Decipher* with seven actors—four men and three women—two of whom would also double as instrumental musicians, each playing the banjo and guitar. All seven performers would also sing in the production, which would feature fourteen different songs—six solos, five duets, and three ensemble numbers involving the entire company. Playwright, lyricist and composer Jan Leander was scheduled to be in residence throughout the rehearsal period for this premier production, making changes as needed.

The cast list was posted on February 3. The first rehearsal was announced for February 4. The production was scheduled to open on March 7. In all, there were only thirty-one days between the first rehearsal and opening night. The calendar looked like this:

	S	M	T	W	T	F	S
FEB	3	4	5	6	7	8	9
	10	11	12	13	14	15	16
	17	18	19	20	21	22	23
	24	25	26	27	28		
MARCH						1	2
	3	4	5	6	7	8	9

The cast was scheduled to rehearse four hours a day (from 10:00 a.m. to noon and from 1:30 p.m. to 3:30 p.m.), seven days a week, from February 4 through February 26, during which time they would also perform nightly in *No Time for Sergeants*. *Sergeants* closed on the twenty-sixth; the next day *American Decipher* would move from a rehearsal hall into the theatre and onto the stage. The first technical rehearsal was scheduled for March 1.

Jones thought the production would run about two hours in length, not counting one fifteen-minute intermission between the two acts.

When, he wondered, should he ask actors to be "off book," to have their lines learned?

Questions

1. What would you advise Jones?

2. What factors influence your advice?

3. How would you decide this question in directing some other production?

CASE 15. A CASTING MISTAKE: *THE GLASS MENAGERIE*

Suzanne Smith, one of two directors in the Cross River Community College theatre program, realized after the third rehearsal of Tennessee Williams' *The Glass Menagerie* that she had made a terrible mistake. Eliza Ambers, the actress she had selected to play Laura, could not possibly play the part and should not have been cast. Not only, Smith thought, would Ambers be unable to perform the role with any semblance of believability, her lack of compatibility with the character would also bring havoc to the entire production. To be sure, Ambers had some talent, even if it wasn't extraordinary, but Smith knew she had made a mistake by casting her in this particular role.

Ambers was a transfer student who had not acted before. While she seemed to be fine during auditions, it took only an evening of reading the entire play and two preliminary rehearsals for Smith to realize that Ambers' voice, a thin, high-pitched monotone, was unacceptable, and that her movements were stilted, awkward and uncomfortable. More importantly, her overall quality seemed to convey strong belligerence and anger, qualities Smith saw as far removed from the character of Laura.

As Smith sat alone in her apartment after the third rehearsal, she considered her options. She could tell Ambers, simply, that a mistake had been made, then recast the role, either by holding further auditions or by asking one of the regular theatre students (none of whom had auditioned for the play) to play the role. She could wait a week or so before doing anything; perhaps, she thought, Ambers would surprise her and get better. She could also just commit herself to doing the play as she had cast it, sticking with Ambers and working with her until opening.

Questions

1. What should Smith do?

2. How would you try to prevent yourself from making this kind of mistake?

3. Under what conditions should an actor be replaced in a role after rehearsals have begun?

CASE 16. GETTING THE "FLOW": *THE PRISONER OF SECOND AVENUE*

As director of the Barnstead Theatre production of Neil Simon's *The Prisoner of Second Avenue,* James Pond looked forward to the remaining time before performances began. Almost one week of the two-and-a-half-week rehearsal period was behind him, and he was enjoying his scheduled day away from the theatre. The break gave him time to assess what should be done in the week ahead.

In general, he thought, the production was going well. His only quandaries concerned John Creech. He worried about Creech as an actor, about what kind of professional relationship seemed to be developing between them, and about Creech's eventual influence on the rest of the cast.

As Pond reflected, his thoughts returned to the most recent rehearsal. He had begun to talk with Creech about evident awkwardness in his movement and blocking when Creech interrupted him, saying, "Don't worry about it. I'm just getting the flow. Don't give me any notes. You see, this is the way I like to work. Let me get the feel of it, just wandering around and exploring. We can get to specifics later."

Each day in the week had been the same. Every time Pond tried to say something to him, Creech interrupted with a variation of the same thought. It began to look like Creech might refuse all direction.

Barnstead theatre

A semi-professional theatre located in a small metropolitan area in Pennsylvania, the Barnstead had been in existence since 1972, and was still operated by the three middle-aged producing directors—Richard Dawn, John Creech and Bruce Montgomery—who had founded it twelve years earlier as a community venture. It occupied the largest part of a downtown Center for the Arts, a building complex which also housed an art gallery, recital hall and various classrooms and work spaces. Plays were staged on the circular thrust stage, surrounded by a fan-shaped auditorium which could seat 250 audience members. Well staffed and equipped, the Barnstead also boasted a full-time, non-union acting company employed on a seasonal basis. (Summer contracts were also available for those actors who wished.) Eight of the actors, along with the producers, had been with the company since its inception. Together, they had built a large audience following, many of whom had become especially attached to the individual actors. Dawn, Creech, Montgomery and three of the actors also taught at a nearby community college.

Each year the theatre produced nine or ten plays in a season that ran from early November through June. Each production enjoyed a two-and-a-half-week rehearsal period, then played seven performances a week for three weeks. The actors, by contract, could rehearse for twenty-eight hours during the first week, then thirty-one hours per week after that. (See the Appendix, in this case, for a typical rehearsal schedule.) All rehearsals were held during the afternoon so as not to conflict with evening performances or morning teaching responsibilities at the college. No rehearsals were held on Thursdays, because of the regularly scheduled matinee. The theatre was dark on Mondays.

The production

When *The Prisoner of Second Avenue* had been selected in September as part of the regular theatre season, Dawn, Creech and Montgomery had decided to break with tradition and hire an outside director for the production. It was the first play in twelve years to be directed by someone other than one of the three founding directors. In October, the three men hired Judy Pond as stage manager for the season. She, in turn, suggested to them that they hire her husband, James, to direct *The Prisoner of Second Avenue.* He was a free-lance director with ten years' experience directing in a variety of theatre situations. By December, James Pond had signed a contract, and the public relations department began publicizing the Barnstead's first guest director.

The Prisoner of Second Avenue features two characters, Mel and Edna Edison, who dominate the play. Alone on stage during all of Act I, they are joined after the first scene of Act II by four other persons. As was usual, Dawn and Montgomery were responsible for casting, and they cast all six roles from their regular company, selecting Creech and Carmen Davenport to play Mel and Edna. Creech, at age 47, and Davenport, 54, had played together frequently before and could share equal strength on stage. Creech, however, objected, arguing that the play needed only one star. He suggested that Edna be played by Nancy Kartin, a twenty-four-year-old heavy-set young actress who had joined the company during its current season. Dawn and Montgomery, after discussing the problem at length, transferred the role to Kartin. They worried about upsetting Creech, whose emotional problems were growing more intense, and whose wife, the Barnstead costumer, had suggested to them privately that he seemed to be on the verge of a nervous breakdown. The men shared none of this information with Pond, but they did tell him, on the day before rehearsal began, that Kartin had been on a rigorous "no food" diet which had helped her lose thirty-five pounds in the last three weeks. "It's a fine cast," said Dawn to Pond, "and everyone is eager to work with an outside director."

Pond began his first rehearsal by talking with the entire cast about the play. He began the second rehearsal by blocking Act I. No sooner had he begun to explain movement patterns to Creech and Kartin than Creech interrupted with "Let's make this a community effort—something we all contribute to. What I'd like to do is just walk around the stage for a while—you know, to get the flow. Just tell me the general area where I should be and let me worry about the specifics. I'll decide those and if what I do doesn't work, I'll change it. I can feel those kind of things fairly easily once I get the flow."

Pond didn't know for sure what "getting the flow" meant, but he let the moment pass. In the time since then he had continued to avoid any confrontation with Creech, even though the whole situation had become increasingly difficult. While the four actors in Act II wanted to be told every small detail, and while Nancy Kartin worried about developing her first major role for Barnstead, Creech went his own way, wandering aimlessly back and forth across the stage as he struggled with the role.

As rehearsals progressed, Pond noticed when he did

manage to give Creech a note, that two or three rehearsal periods would pass before Creech responded. Then he would try what Pond had suggested. Rejection of suggestions, however, usually came quickly. Occasionally, when Pond would begin to correct something in a scene, Creech would say, "You don't have to tell me anything. I know what I did wrong." Only once did Creech seem bitter, and he turned to Pond, angrily saying, "No! I won't do it that way."

Creech's negative reactions, at first, had seemed limited to the areas of blocking. As rehearsals progressed, however, they extended to rhythm, pace and, especially, intensity. Creech played everything at a high level, losing entirely the subtlety Pond saw needed for the role. Eager for an excellent production, however, Pond was patient. Changing behavior patterns that had developed over a twelve-year period, he knew, would be difficult, if not impossible. And at least Creech seemed to be working hard; in fact, other cast members were surprised at his progress. He was known for tardiness in learning lines, for example, and already he knew them for *The Prisoner of Second Avenue.*

Yet Pond knew erratic blocking, distorted rhythm and false intensity could destroy other production elements with little difficulty, and he wondered, when rehearsals began again the next day, just how he should approach the problem.

Questions

1. Analyze Pond's situation at the Barnstead Theatre.

2. How should Pond handle John Creech?

3. What other recommendations would you make to Pond at this point?

CASE 16. APPENDIX

Rehearsal Schedule: The Prisoner of Second Avenue

Barnstead Theatre

Saturday	1–3	Wednesday	1–5
Sunday	1–5	Thursday	
Monday	2–6	Friday	1–5
Tuesday	1–5	Saturday	1–3
Wednesday	1–5	Sunday	11–1 and 2:00 Technical Rehearsal
Thursday			
Friday	1–5	Monday	10:00 Tech/ Dress and 2:00 Dress Rehearsal
Saturday	1–3		
Sunday	1–5	Tuesday	Opening Night
Monday	2–6		
Tuesday	1–5		

CASE 17. COMPANY RULES: *THE TEMPEST*

Aaron Gold was directing a production of *The Tempest* for a small community theatre in the urban heart of New Orleans. The first technical rehearsal—which was also the first rehearsal for which company members would "sign in" and proceed as if under performance conditions—was scheduled for less than a week in the future. Gold had agreed to work with Tammy Neil, the stage manager, on a list of "company rules" for posting on the call-board at that time. These rules, all had agreed, would govern company behavior during the dress rehearsals and performances.

As Gold prepared for a meeting with Neil to discuss this issue, he hastily scribbled down some potential ideas:

1. Please sign in nightly.
2. If for some reason you will be late for call, please telephone Tammy Neil at xxx-xxxx or at the theatre, xxx-xxxx.
3. Please leave your valuables at home, secure them in your locker or give them to the assistant stage manager for safekeeping.
4. Please keep the make-up room and the dressing rooms clean.
5. Please come to the theatre only through the backstage door; do not use the lobby entrance.
6. Visitors are welcome in the green room after the performance but not before then.
7. Please respond to the stage manager when she announces call times with "Thank you."
8. Do not flush the toilet during the performance, only before curtain, after the curtain call, and at intermission.
9. Please notify the ticket office daily about the disposition of your two complimentary tickets for each performance.
10. Please smoke only on the loading platform, never indoors.

Gold knew he had just begun. He also knew that this list of company rules would be different from the rules at other theatres where he had worked.

Questions

1. What would you add to Gold's beginning list?

2. What rules might be different for a community theatre? A university theatre? A professional theatre? A children's theatre?

3. Do you think it is desirable to have such company rules for a production? Why or why not?

CASE 18. MOVE-IN: *THE SILENT SONG*

The Phoenix Rising Theatre Company world premier production of Allen Stalker's *The Silent Song* was evolving into a complex two-and-one-half-hour production that would feature forty-seven individual scenes performed by six actors and actresses on a spacious and open set designed to suggest an aging, crumbling European waterfront dock. Two stories in height, the set would eventually stretch thirty-five feet into the fly space and feature eleven distinct playing areas separated by a complicated system of ramps, ladders, steps and bridges. Each of the areas would be used by itself and in combination with one or more of the other areas. The six actors would play more than thirty roles.

Planned so that all of the performers would remain on stage at all times, even when they were not directly participating in a given scene, the talented cast rehearsed for four weeks on the flat floor of a cramped third-story walk-up hall about one-half the size of the eventual playing space. So small was the rehearsal space, in fact, that the ground plans for extreme stage left and stage right acting areas were actually taped on the walls rather than the floor. Since the ceiling in this room was only nine feet high, different elevations for the set were indicated by different colored tape on the floor. Two-by-six lumber, nailed flat to the floor, indicated steps or ladders; silver duct tape suggested the various ramps and bridges.

When the company finally moved to the stage from the rehearsal hall, the set was complete, and two full rehearsals remained before the scheduled technical rehearsal, which would be followed by three dress rehearsals and opening night. Rehearsals were limited to four hours each day because of other commitments in the theatre.

Question

1. Prepare a rehearsal schedule for the first on-stage rehearsal of *The Silent Song*. Analyze this schedule.

Chapter IV   Working with Actors

CASE 19. THE INDIVIDUAL ACTOR: ONLY TEN MINUTES TO BUFFALO

Director Carol Simpson studied her promptbook late Wednesday evening after rehearsal and realized anew that her production of *Only Ten Minutes to Buffalo,* a one-act play by Günter Grass, opened in two days. Six performances were scheduled—on Friday, Saturday and Sunday evenings for the next two weekends—and ticket sales were going well. Considerable audience enthusiasm for the play had been generated, primarily because of Simpson's well-publicized unusual treatment of the script and her past reputation as a director.

Throughout the short three-week rehearsal period she had faced many problems. None of them, however, were so demanding as those presented by Karl Roper, an actor appearing in his first play. Roper had bewildered her almost from the beginning, and she was to meet him on Thursday morning at ten o'clock for a final individual rehearsal. Simpson knew that before then she had to decide how best to handle the developing situation. She also knew that Thursday would be the day before performance.

Background

Only Ten Minutes to Buffalo was being staged as part of the Studio Theatre Season at the University of Lindigen, a large and cosmopolitan state university noted nationally for its theatre programs. Carol Simpson, a twenty-four-year-old Ph.D. candidate in theatre, had directed three previous productions at Lindigen, and had also directed several plays at two other universities. In accordance with Studio Theatre Season established policy, she had selected the play, discussed its production with the Studio Theatre Board of Directors (gaining enthusiastic approval from this group of theatre faculty and students), scheduled it with careful regard for University and departmental regulations, and held auditions open to the entire campus.

The open auditions had required special Studio Board approval, because participation in such productions was

102

usually limited to undergraduate and graduate majors in theatre, plus those additional students currently registered for theatre courses.

After casting the five male and two female roles, plus a chorus of two additional people she had written into the play herself, Simpson gathered the actors together for a first rehearsal. In addition to having the cast read through the script, she discussed with them her approach to the play, and she talked briefly about the process of rehearsal. As she explained it, rehearsals would be held seven days a week, but most actors would have to attend only three times, as called, because she had divided the play into small rehearsal units of scenes between different characters. The chorus, too, could be rehearsed separately in this manner, even though eventually it would be integral to every scene. Every fourth day or so the entire cast would be called for a run-through of the hour-long script and for some collective exercises designed to help build a sense of togetherness and ensemble, which Simpson thought was important for the production. She also explained that the final week prior to performances would require everybody's presence.

Rehearsals began with blocking, then moved to intense work on characterization, followed by several sessions devoted primarily to rhythm and timing. Throughout, Simpson relied heavily on vocal and physical exercises, theatre games and improvisations, as well as on concentrated work with the script. After a few polishing rehearsals, the cast and crews went into technical and dress rehearsals. Except for Roper, the actors and the production seemed ready for performance. Roper's work, however, proved so erratic that Simpson worried about his effect on the total production.

Karl Roper

Karl Roper celebrated his 40th birthday one week before auditions for *Only Ten Minutes to Buffalo*. A junior college graduate, he had spent several years in the army, then had worked for a while before enrolling at Lindigen. This was his first semester back in school and he had looked forward to beginning again. Since he was registered for a four-hour

Theatre Practicum course which required twenty hours of work each week in the theatre, it seemed only natural that he audition for a play. Though he had never acted before, he was delighted to be cast by Simpson as Kotschenreuther in *Only Ten Minutes to Buffalo*. A small but critical role, it seemed "artsy" and exciting, and Roper thought it small enough to handle while open enough to provide opportunity for "hamming it up."

Roper was surprised, however, to learn that most rehearsals would begin at 11 p.m. and last until 12:30 or 1:00 in the morning, a schedule designed to accommodate the other theatre activity of several cast members. While he expressed concern to Simpson about staying up that late, he also wanted the credit, and he needed the hours to complete his Practicum. Furthermore, he felt the role of an eccentric painter suited him well. During the rehearsal period he rarely talked to other members of the cast, all of whom noted as time went on that Roper always dressed in the same clothes and always wanted to be left alone when not actually on stage. Once, when he appeared late for a rehearsal, Simpson talked to him afterwards, asking "Why were you late?" His response puzzled her: "Don't try to understand me," he said, "you're much too young and too naive ever to understand me. I'm too deep."

Midway through the second week of rehearsal Simpson realized that Roper was having trouble remembering his blocking. Rehearsals of scenes in which he appeared began to take longer while Simpson patiently helped him. She even scheduled special rehearsal sessions for him, during which they worked not only on blocking, but also on characterization and vocal strength. (Only occasionally could Roper be heard further than halfway back in the small theatre.) During these sessions he worked hard, moved and spoke well, but experienced trouble in repeating anything a second time. Since he could not remember what he had done, he told Simpson, he couldn't duplicate it. Simpson was patient, and Roper always seemed willing to listen; he responded with seeming eagerness to her attempts to help him improve.

After Wednesday's rehearsal Simpson had asked Roper to stay for yet another individual session. When the other cast members had left, she said to him: "You know, I can't help you in performance. When you forget things that destroy a scene, when you don't bring the properties on stage as we've rehearsed, when you always play facing-upstage, when you talk so softly that no one can hear you—these are things that in performance I can't do anything to make better."

"You're right," responded Roper, "but it doesn't matter what you say—tonight or all the other nights. In performance it's what the actor does that's important; what he does is what happens on stage. Don't worry. I'll be fine—even though I'll do things in performance that you've never seen before. It will be good. Don't worry."

Simpson, taken aback, arranged to meet him in the morning, then went home.

Questions

1. What should Simpson do when she meets Roper in the morning?

2. As Simpson, what do you consider the major problems, if any, to be? What steps would you take to resolve them?

3. At what points, if any, might corrective actions have been taken to avoid the problems?

CASE 20. THE SINGLE SCENE: *PICNIC*

Director Maria Woodrung stood quietly alone on stage. Rehearsal for the evening was over, and the cast for William Inge's *Picnic* had left the building. As she enjoyed the quiet of an empty theatre, Woodrung thought back over the first two weeks of rehearsal. The production, produced by Bartley Conservatory, had grown rapidly, exceeding her highest expectations. Yet one problem had persisted, and from her perspective it had seemed easy to identify: every time the two actresses who played the teachers in Act II came on stage for their short scene together, everything fell apart. The scene was a disaster, and it managed to drop the bottom out of an otherwise excellent production.

Woodrung had been sure the source of the problem was equally easy to identify: the entire matter seemed the fault of Jackie Bonderin, a black actress who played one of the teachers. Bonderin seemed to resent the smallness of the role and the idea of working with a non-black director. Furthermore, Woodrung thought, Bonderin apparently resented the seeming "tokenism" of being cast in such a role. As rehearsals had progressed, Bonderin had grown less and less responsive, more and more disruptive. Her attitude had also begun to influence Barbara Calder, the young actress who played the other teacher. The situation had grown steadily worse. Though it had yet to explode in any major way, it smoldered as an undercurrent that had begun to affect the entire company.

Background

Founded in the mid-1960's as a professional training school for college-aged theatre artists, Bartley Conservatory offered a high-level training program for potential actors, designers and technicians. Four years of concentrated study led to a B.F.A. degree, and graduated students had been very successful in finding theatre-related employment. Some, in fact, found positions in the year-round professional company operated by the Conservatory itself.

Maria Woodrung, age 51, had been a teacher and director

for the Conservatory since its inception, and over the years she had developed into a beloved and excellent mentor. Students adored her. An outstanding director, she tempered high goals and demands for excellence with kindness, patience and understanding. Students knew she cared; consequently, they worked hard when cast in productions she directed.

Picnic was the Conservatory's second mainstage production of the 1982–83 season, and partly because Woodrung was the director, many students attended the General Auditions, a screening try-out held before each Bartley production. When Woodrung had prepared a call-back list, she shared it with several faculty colleagues, as was usual practice for the professional faculty directors. One of them asked her why the names of no black students appeared on the list. She responded that black actors seemed inappropriate for *Picnic,* a play set in rural Kansas during the 1950's. When he pointed out that she might be wrong, that "color-blind" casting might, indeed, work for certain roles in the play, and that perhaps her omission was more a sign of latent prejudice than artistic judgment, she agreed, immediately adding the names of two black students to the list. Both students had demonstrated at General Auditions and by previous work that they were capable and talented, real possibilities for the cast of *Picnic.* In fact, during the final audition reading Woodrung decided that one of them, Jackie Bonderin, should play one of the teachers in Act II.

Bonderin and Barbara Calder were both sophomore theatre majors. Each had survived the 50 percent cut of students at the end of their freshman year; each also knew that one-third of their current class would not be invited to return as juniors. For both of them, the roles in *Picnic* were important. Since freshmen were prohibited from acting, and since sophomores rarely received more than one role (always minor) in a mainstage production, the play offered their only public opportunity to prove to faculty, including Woodrung, that they should continue study in acting. Each approached the production, therefore, with real seriousness. They were especially glad to be working with Woodrung; not only should that mean an excellent production, they knew her word carried special weight in the usual evaluation process.

Soon after the four-and-a-half-week rehearsal period began, it became apparent that the production would be even better than Bartley's usual level of excellence. The happy combination of talented actors, well directed, brought unusual depth to rehearsal; the cast congealed as an ensemble very early.

Only one point in the play presented problems: the small scene between the two teachers in Act II. Woodrung had asked herself repeatedly, "Why is the scene there?" But no ready answer had presented itself. Since the scene was short, however, and since it seemed to have little impact on the rest of the play, she felt confident the company would be able to get through it without difficulty.

Jackie Bonderin and Barbara Calder had begun well. Their small accomplishment in the first few rehearsals, however, gradually disappeared, replaced by an awkwardness that didn't work at all. Both students were talented actresses, among the best in the sophomore class, but their best efforts produced only slim results. Their scene floundered. Gradually they became separated from the rest of the cast, whose sympathy toward them only brought an increased sense of failure. (Once, after a rehearsal, Calder stopped to apologize to the rest of the cast for "letting everyone down.") Both students grew more and more worried about their roles as rehearsals progressed; their fellow cast members worried with them.

Through these beginning weeks of rehearsal Woodrung also worried. Yet she kept reminding herself, "After all, it's only two small roles in a very short scene." She was sure that sooner or later something would help the scene get better.

Midway through the rehearsal period Woodrung began to work more specifically with each of the two actresses, eventually exhausting her resources of technical devices. She led them in improvising actions, gave them props to use, devised costume pieces for them to handle, urged them into grotesque character exaggerations, even tried side-coaching. Nothing seemed to work. The harder she pressed, the worse they became. As the problem grew, Woodrung began to cut the scene, shortening it in order to strengthen the total play. Ten lines apiece for the two characters became only seven, then five.

As the special rehearsals grew in intensity, Woodrung began to think that Bonderin was using stored-up resentment to sabotage the play. At first, she pushed the idea from her mind: Bonderin was too good, too professional in attitude, for such behavior. Nevertheless, something had to account for Bonderin's strange attitude, and Woodrung grew increasingly convinced that the black actress was letting her blackness, consciously or not, destroy her performance.

Bonderin's attitude, Woodrung sensed, had begun to rub off on Calder. Soon both actresses began to ignore given directions, frequently appeared late for rehearsal call, and generally began creating problems greater than just lack of character and scene development. Woodrung saw lethargy creep into their performances, and could not stop it.

Woodrung talks to the stage manager

Alone on stage, in the silence of the deserted theatre, Woodrung recalled her conversation a few minutes earlier with Dwight Longstreet, stage manager for the production. Only tonight, after a particularly trying rehearsal, had she finally asked if he knew what was going wrong. His reply had shocked her: "Neither Jackie nor Barbara are upset at all by this 'blackness' thing, even though they think you probably are. What bothers them is they have no idea what they're doing or why they're doing it, or even why their characters are in the play. They feel lost—small and insignificant—like the characters they play. They also know how awful you think their scene is, and they're really upset about disappointing you so much."

Woodrung felt devastated. "It's my fault," she thought. "It's my fault and not theirs at all. All this time I've been blaming Jackie and her influence on Barbara, sure that this black actress playing her first mainstage role was using her black-ness as a shield to keep the play and the character at arm's length. Instead, it's been me—my sending unconscious signals to them that the roles, and the actresses playing them, were insignificant. They were getting the message, and they responded to it accordingly. Now what do I do?"

Woodrung knew she had to correct the misunderstanding as soon as possible. While knowing the problem was hers, she also realized that Bonderin and Calder were equally sure the fault was theirs. Communication between actresses and director, of course, had become strained.

Questions

1. Analyze this situation and the developments that created it.

2. How could the problems, if any, have been avoided?

3. What should Woodrung do?

CASE 21. THE INEXPERIENCED ACTOR: *MARAT/SADE*

John Elan was a first-year theatre student at Valpaso College and had been cast—primarily because of his pleasant demeanor and his considerable if untrained talent—as Marat, one of two title roles in Peter Weiss's *Marat/Sade*. The most ambitious theatre project at Valpaso in several years, the production featured forty-five actors, an enormous and complex playing space, and the full instrumental ensemble suggested by the musical score.

Three weeks into the five-week rehearsal period, just eight days before dress rehearsals were scheduled to begin, director Emmett Cubbins had begun to be concerned about Elan's inexperience. While Elan showed moments of real truth in rehearsal, and while he worked exceptionally hard and seriously, Elan was becoming increasingly inconsistent from one rehearsal to the next. Excellent moments seemingly could not be repeated consistently. Growth one day seemingly would be forgotten the next. Characterization that seemed to work would give way to new and often futile explorations. Even vocal patterns fluctuated with apparently random motivation. In short, Cubbins never knew what to expect next, and he fretted about sustaining growth over the next two weeks and during the scheduled eight performances.

Cubbins worried especially about what seemed to be three special problem areas for Elan. First, his sense of character seemed to be increasingly elusive. Marat would "show up" for one rehearsal, then vanish completely for the next rehearsal. Elan seemed unable to recapture at will the qualities that seemed to work. Each rehearsal was like beginning virtually anew. Second, Elan's very ability to read lines with consistent meaning seemed somehow impaired. Emphasis, for example, and meaning with it, changed with every repetition of a scene. And Elan didn't seem to hear the difference. Third, Elan seemed incapable of consistently conveying mood from the stage to the auditorium. During one moment, for example, Marat's anguish would be unrelenting; in the next moment anguish seemed forgotten, replaced by matter-of-factness more appropriate in an early reading rehearsal.

Even while he worried about these things, Cubbins also

111

thought that perhaps he was overreacting, that perhaps Elan was merely facing the normal struggles of growth during rehearsal. For his part, Elan knew that Cubbins was concerned, and his own frustration was increasing daily.

Questions

1. What advice would you give to Cubbins at this point?

2. What advice would you give to Elan at this point?

3. How would you help an inexperienced, inconsistent actor who lacks training but who has talent?

CASE 22. THE ENSEMBLE: *THE QUEEN SELLERS*

Introduction

Though *The Queen Sellers* had opened some time earlier and had been running successfully off off Broadway in New York, director Lucy Bindlefield remained essentially unsatisfied with the production. She thought her work, rather than finished, had merely entered a new phase. To her a play was a living, breathing thing, subject to change; it needed continual testing and checking, even after it was in performance. She knew, too, that this play had been particularly difficult, and that its quality had deteriorated since opening night. Consequently, she gathered her all-male cast together in the theatre following one evening performance and began a late-night rehearsal with these words: "Well, you've pretty much managed to destroy the whole thing. Everything we worked for. The timing has gone. The rhythm has vanished. The comic business has become burlesque slapstick. And what has happened to the atmosphere, the tension? You've got to stop overacting, stop treating the audience like idiots, stop being so selfish in your roles. You're all playing alone. What's happened to the ensemble? To that sense of togetherness we worked for?"

Her speech led into a three-hour rehearsal, after which she went home to ponder the process by which *The Queen Sellers* had reached its current status. Though she had been directing for almost twenty years, she knew that her rehearsal techniques could develop even further before her next production.

Brief background

Produced by the Actors Theatre Workshop, an influential American theatre company founded by Lucy Bindlefield in 1972, *The Queen Sellers,* while not the theatre's first commercial success, did help fulfill its goal of providing theatre with contemporary relevance for blue-collar audiences. Set in a prison on the night before a planned riot, the play presented a series of comic and serious vignettes dealing with a wide cross-section of prison life.

The entire production showed Bindlefield's touch as a director. She had begun her theatre career in the 1960's, and her efforts with the workshop had achieved international recognition. In *The Queen Sellers* Bindlefield had used all the accumulated knowledge and experience which had, over the years, developed into a widely recognized and somewhat unusual approach to directing.

The production process: auditions and early rehearsals

Actors in *The Queen Sellers* were unaccustomed to Bindlefield's method of work, for none had worked with her previously. Yet she spent little time explaining her approach or its goals, preferring instead to let the work be judged by its results. Straightforward, direct, often embarrassingly honest, Bindlefield tackled *The Queen Sellers* with her usual energy and verve.

At auditions, only one man at a time was permitted to enter the room where Bindlefield waited. She met each one individually, then handed him a script, saying, "Read all the parts; play all the characters." Some began immediately. Others hesitated or asked for further explanation; Bindlefield responded with "Go ahead. Do it. Either you're an actor or you aren't." Each actor then attempted to portray a collage of characters, reading cold from the unfamiliar script. For most, it proved a first-time experience, and when she asked, each thought he had read poorly. Some, in fact, argued that such an exercise made them feel more like an idiot than an actor. Bindlefield countered these feelings by saying, "Well, at least you're willing to look silly—and any good actor must be willing to do that."

When she had thus interviewed each of the auditionees individually, she called some of them back for a further reading. After gathering them all together on stage, she said, "Just wander around now. Sit, if you like. And talk to each other. I'll watch what you do." After an hour she interrupted them, then cast the play immediately.

Rehearsals began an hour later.

During the first week the actors worked without scripts. None had even read the play. They knew only that it was about prison life, and that it was peopled by both prisoners and guards. Because none of the actors had ever been in prison and could only imagine what it might be like, Bindlefield began by attempting to create the prison environment—the narrow world of steel and stone, the open cells and high windows, the sound of metal and silence, the love/hate relationship between guard and prisoner, the daily gossip, the jealousy and intrigue—all the things, she explained, that make up the routine of boredom and festering emotion.

After improvisations and role-playing for several days, she led the cast to the rooftop of a nearby building. Once there, she had them form a circle, in silence, then walk, imagining themselves to be prisoners out on exercise. Round and round they trudged (for what to the actors, it was later reported, seemed like hours), stopping now and then to be permitted a cigarette and brief conversation, then back into the circle for more exercise. Bindlefield hope the experience would help them capture the boredom and meanness of prison routine. She continued it for several days.

Next, and still on the roof, she had the cast improvise what she called "A Day in Prison." It began with a cell-block security check at morning call, then included washing out cells, marching to breakfast, eating in silence—and on and on through an entire day. This improvisation developed over several rehearsal days, and as it became more elaborate, Bindlefield began to introduce actual situations from the script. Consequently, when the actors were finally told several weeks later which specific roles they would be playing, they often discovered that situations which had been improvised actually occurred in the play.

The production process: rehearsal methods

By the time scripts were distributed Bindlefield had broken the play down into units, each a very short scene, each with a beginning, middle and end. Some of the units were only a few lines long, but in each one the actor, or actors, had a specific objective to work toward. In the first act of *The Queen Sellers,* for example, there was a big scene set in the prison library, where the prisoners were marched on, then permitted a ten-minute break during which they secretively made final plans for the riot. The scene was built up slowly during four weeks of rehearsal. The different small units within the scene—the sharing of a cigarette, the passing of a knife, the seemingly aimless fight—were rehearsed individually and built gradually into the whole. In performance, most of these small units would take less than a minute, but Bindlefield rehearsed them endlessly, over and over again. She rehearsed each unit in the play with similar care.

Frequently during this time, Bindlefield would collect the actors' scripts and ask them again to improvise. In fact, she rarely let a rehearsal day pass without spending half the time in improvisation. Often the physical movement which accompanied such exercises was then modified for use in the production itself, for the director never actually blocked the play from any prearranged notions. Rather, she hoped the patterns of movement and the groupings of characters would grow out of the characters themselves.

The combination of detail work coupled with improvisation lasted until opening night, when *The Queen Sellers* met with instant success and won critical acclaim for its acting and directing.

Questions

1. Analyze the directing techniques used by Lucy Bindlefield. From what she did during rehearsal, what seems important to her?

2. If Bindlefield were to consult with you prior to beginning her next production, what would you advise?

CASE 23. INJURY: *WOYZECK*

Director John Rich could sense from his aisle seat in the back row of the darkened theatre that this particular performance of Georg Büchner's *Woyzeck* was going exceptionally well.

The cast, playing its fifth of eight consecutive and sold-out performances, was in the middle of Scene XVI, and only twenty-five minutes remained before the final curtain. At the end of the scene, actor Keith Klevins, who played the title character, leapt from a twelve-foot-high scaffolding, as blocked. The lights faded perfectly, blacking out just as he landed on the stage floor. The effect, Rich thought, was spectacular: the character seemed to vanish into darkness before he stopped falling.

Seven seconds of planned silence would pass, Rich knew, before the company of twenty actors would begin to hum softly in the dark. Then Klevins would begin to speak, cueing the lights to fade up slowly for the next scene.

The humming began. But Klevins didn't speak. No lights came on. Seven seconds stretched to twenty, then to thirty, then to forty-five. Rich worried that the audience would grow impatient and break the penetrating mood that had completely engulfed them since early in the performance. Just as he began to fear that something must have gone wrong, the house manager appeared at his side, whispering quietly, "They need you backstage."

He left quickly through a rear door, then ran around the building to the stage entrance. In the hallway which connected to off-stage right he saw Klevins sitting on the floor, with Carol Clarke, the excellent stage manager, hovering over him. His right arm, cut open from elbow to wrist, lay limply on his legs.

Clarke explained quickly that when Klevins had jumped from the scaffolding his arm had caught on an exposed bolt, ripping it open as he fell. Rich realized that Klevins had left the stage during the black-out to find Clarke, who then delayed the next light cue. Miraculously, Klevins seemed alert, calm and without pain; there was little blood.

Background

Woyzeck had been produced by Millenville University, a small, midwestern, liberal arts college, that enrolled approximately 1200 students and had a strong theatre program noted for its experimental work. John Rich, at age thirty-two, had been an energetic and creative member of the faculty for seven years; he also served as Director of Theatre.

Woyzeck was the fourth play in Millenville's series of five major productions. An open script with multiple short scenes, the play was incomplete when playwright Büchner died in the early 1800's, and Rich had arranged the disconnected scenes into what he considered a unique dramatic whole, then had cast an ensemble of twenty actors to play the seventy-four identifiable roles. Only Woyzeck and his wife, Marie, plus Karl, the village idiot, were played by actors without other roles. All of the actors were onstage during the entire production.

The resulting production was an environmental collage performed on a sculptured jungle-gym setting that encompassed both playing areas and space for an audience of one hundred persons. Most of the action took place above the stage floor, demanding of the actors considerable skill in gymnastic movement. The title role was especially athletic: Woyzeck spent most of his time on the bars, traveling from one area to another with a series of acrobatic moves whose ease of execution belied their difficulty. The total effect was of a cockeyed and distorted circus, in which cruelty, violence and joy were exaggerated in a style reminiscent of expressionism.

Keith Klevins

The skilled cast had grown unusually close during the process of their preparation, partially because the play demanded such high levels of concentration and precision. Throughout the long six-week rehearsal period Klevins had been the acknowledged leader, not only as the title character, but also as the most experienced and most athletic of the cast. A senior theatre major, he was a cautious, disciplined and highly talented actor who had appeared in eighteen previous Millenville productions and was committed to pursuing acting as a career.

Rich looked as Klevins stared at his arm and knew that something had to be done. The wound appeared to start at the bend in Klevins' elbow, then traced downward across the muscle to his wrist. Although the skin was spread open, he could not tell for sure how serious the injury was. Rich could hear the actors still humming in the dark on stage; none of them, like the audience, had seen Klevins leave the stage.

More than a minute passed as Rich analyzed the situation. The audience had been in the dark for some one hundred and twenty seconds. Clarke suggested that Klevins should go to the hospital immediately; the play should be stopped and the audience invited to attend a later production. Klevins argued that he felt fine; he wanted to wrap the arm in an Ace bandage from the first-aid kit and continue the performance; he could go to the doctor or emergency room in half an hour.

Rich knew that these were not the only two options. He also knew that some decision had to be made quickly.

Questions

1. Analyze Rich's options and the consequences of each.

2. Which option should Rich choose? Why?

CASE 24. GIVING AND TAKING NOTES: HUNTSVILLE THEATRE

As a director at the Huntsville Theatre, Miriam Wellingham had thought often about the process of communicating with her collaborators, and she knew that, by and large, once a production had begun, her skill at taking and giving "notes" was of critical importance to that process. Her notes, she knew, were the means by which her ideas were shared with others.

Wellingham thought especially about her communication with actors during and after each rehearsal period, and she knew she must be clear—to herself and to the performers—about at least three different things.

First, she had to deal with what she thought of as the journalistic matters:

a) what to say
b) when to say it
c) how to say it
d) where to say it
e) who to say it to, and finally,
f) why it should be said at all.

Second, she needed to reinforce for herself an idea she knew was true: "What I say is not always what they hear."

Third, she knew she needed to explain to actors her own idiosyncrasies in giving and taking notes. Every director is different in this regard, she thought, and helping actors understand her own individuality would help her communicate with them more effectively. "What does it mean, for example, when I give lots of notes after a rehearsal instead of only a few?" she thought. "What does it mean when, early in the rehearsal process, I interrupt scene work to give notes? What does it mean—" and she thought of all the other factors that influenced her own approach to taking and giving notes.

In the end, Wellingham knew that the quality of her directing would be a direct result of the quality of her communication skills. She resolved to understand better her own work.

Questions

1. How do you respond to what Wellingham calls the "journalistic" matters of note giving and taking?

2. How do you help insure that what people here is what you intend to say?

3. What are your idiosyncrasies in the giving and taking of notes? Would you consider these strengths or weaknesses? How do they affect your rehearsal process? How would you let a cast know about them?

CASE 25. PERFORMANCE INCONSISTENCY:
THE GOOD WOMAN OF SETZUAN

Bertolt Brecht's *The Good Woman of Setzuan,* as produced by the undergraduate theatre program at Olympia College, was scheduled for eighteen performances over a six-week period, playing Thursday through Saturday each week-end. While experienced and well-trained senior theatre majors played the roles of Shen-Te, the prostitute, and Wong, the Water Seller, the remaining twenty-three actors were primarily first- and second-year students who had not yet studied acting. Most, in fact, were appearing in their first play. As the play finished its sixth performance, director Daniel Barnes knew that the production had begun to deteriorate, that the cast was straying further and further from the excellent performance of opening night. What had then been crisp and careful characterization had somehow become sloppy and lazy caricature; what had been superb pacing had gradually become laborious slowness; what had been an intimate, interesting sense of communication had become a bland recitation. Professional actors, Barnes thought, could sustain a production over this extended period of time by drawing on their craft, their technique. His actors, because of their age and inexperience, had no such tools.

Questions

1. What should Barnes do?

2. Assume you have called one or more special rehearsals to deal with this problem. What would you do during these rehearsals?

3. How would you guard against such inconsistency and deterioration in the weeks ahead?

4. Could Barnes have prevented this problem? If so, how?

CASE 26. ILLNESS: *WHERE HAS TOMMY FLOWERS GONE?* (A)

Director Richard Fransk sat talking with his stage manager, Beverly Jamison, late in the evening following a Tuesday night rehearsal in July of 1986. They agreed that *Where Has Tommy Flowers Gone?* was in trouble. Part of the summer repertory season produced by Climata Community College, the play had been rushed since its beginning, partially because only thirteen rehearsals had been scheduled between auditions and the opening performance. Now the leading actor and actress had missed almost a week of rehearsal. The production had reached crisis point.

"We open on Thursday night," said Jamison, a thirty-year-old former student who, in addition to her responsibilities as stage manager, also played a small role in the play. "That's just three days from now. You must decide what to do, and you must also decide when to do it."

"Yes," said Fransk. "But at this point my options seem limited. It's like all the directing textbooks say: I have an obligation to the play, to the audience, to the cast and to myself, but there's no way to please everybody. And how will the administration respond?"

"Nevertheless," Jamison replied, "you've only got two rehearsals left. I say kick them out and recast, live with them regardless of the results, or figure out a way to work around them. What else can you do?"

Fransk agreed they should decide before each went home. He also wondered what other options might be available.

Background

Located in a large, midwestern city, Climata Community College enrolled more than 20,000 students each year. Founded in 1962, it competed with a long established, even larger community college, Bitera, located just four miles away across town. The two schools were different in many ways, but the contrast in theatre activity was especially great. Bitera, established in 1888, enjoyed a long tradition of cultural activity, highlighted by a theatre program that encompassed outstanding facilities, a large student population, seven theatre faculty members and an active production program that included a summer season of five plays. Climata, on the other hand, had limited facilities, very few theatre students, only two theatre faculty and a limited production schedule. Plays were staged in the theatre shop, a converted classroom, that was usually arranged as a modified proscenium.

Dr. Joseph May had taught theatre and directed plays for Climata since the school had begun its limited theatre program in 1977. Richard Fransk had joined the staff in 1980. Young, energetic and well-trained in both educational and professional theatre, Fransk shared with May the responsibilities for theatre program administration and artistic direction. Both men hoped to build a theatre program of excellence, one that could serve the needs of Climata's students while also appealing to the surrounding community.

Summer repertory

Midway through the 1985–86 academic year, after consultation with several persons from the community, May and Fransk decided that Climata should begin a summer season of plays scheduled to correspond with the regular 1986 summer semester. They would each direct one play, and each play would also be considered a course offered by the theatre division during the summer term. The two men agreed with Climata's administration that faculty salaries would be drawn directly from tuition provided by students enrolled in the courses. Each course, therefore, had to attract at least twenty students in order to pay the two faculty members a full summer salary. May and Fransk also agreed that all production expenses would have to be met by box-office income derived from ticket sales.

May and Fransk talked about the risks involved. They agreed that box-office income presented no problem: sufficient revenue could be generated to provide for a minimal production effort. The gamble on student enrollment, however, seemed greater, for if the minimum forty students failed to register, one of the courses would be dropped. In such an event, the two agreed they would divide equally a single salary. May and Fransk also agreed on an organizational plan for the summer. Each class would work independently of the other, and each would produce one of the two plays. There would be no double casting, no double enrollment. This meant, they knew, that each cast must have at least twenty actors, who would also provide what limited technical support became necessary. Each play would be performed three times, alternating in repertory on Friday and Saturday nights over a three-week period corresponding to the last three weeks of the five-and-a-half-week summer session. Classes would end on the Wednesday following the final performance, so there would be adequate time to strike. The opening schedule of registration, auditions and beginning organization left only a thirteen-day rehearsal period.

In addition to directing, May and Fransk agreed to divide production responsibilities for the summer program. Consequently, Fransk, who would direct *Where Has Tommy Flowers Gone?*, would also assume all administrative duties, including box office and publicity. May, while directing the second play, would also function as technical director.

Where has Tommy Flowers gone?

Fransk prepared for auditions by enlarging the flexible cast size from a minimum of six to the twenty he hoped to use, rewriting as necessary so that each actor would have at least one line. On the day of registration, however, only nineteen people registered for the *Tommy Flowers* course. Fransk, after further searching, finally convinced one student to enroll her mother, which brought the class size to the needed twenty.

The total cast, Fransk felt, was weak, filled with inexperienced actors, many of whom were ill cast in specific roles. Yet the play revolved primarily around two central characters, Tommy and Netta, and these roles were filled with capable people. John Sprite, who had graduated from Climata several years earlier, would play Tommy, the disenchanted rebel. Martha Feathering, who lived with Sprite, would play Netta, the girl with whom Tommy discovers true love. Feathering, at age 23, was three years younger than Sprite. Both were well suited for their roles, and both had considerable previous acting experience. Fransk, in fact, had worked with Feathering (although not with Sprite) on several previous productions, and had found her to be hardworking, trustworthy and very talented. Sprite seemed to share similar qualities. Better actors than these, Fransk knew, were not available, and he rejoiced in the strength they would bring to the production.

Because more than half the cast worked full time during the day, rehearsals were scheduled for three hours each evening.

On the morning after the fifth rehearsal Sprite telephoned Fransk to report he had come down with strep throat, had been to see a doctor and had been ordered to bed for a day or two.

"I'll miss tonight's rehearsal," he said, "and probably tomorrow's, too. But I've got the script here and I'll keep studying the role. Maybe I can really get the lines down since I won't be going to work."

The next morning Fransk received a telephone call from Feathering. She, too, was sick and confined to bed. Furthermore, she reported, Sprite seemed worse. Neither of them could speak above a whisper. The doctor had assured them, however, that they should be well enough for rehearsal the following night.

"We'll work on the play together," said Feathering. "I mean, we're both here, so we can cue each other easily. When we get back we shouldn't be very far behind everybody else."

Daily telephone calls between Fransk and the couple followed, but neither seemed to be getting well. Each day they reported a need to miss "just one more rehearsal." Finally, after Sprite had missed four nights, Fransk asked, "Should I replace you? How long, really, will the two of you be gone?"

"We'll be back in just a couple of days," reported Sprite. "And don't worry. We've been working on lines and blocking, as well as on our roles. Everything is coming along fine."

Despite such assurances, Fransk worried more with each day that passed. The rest of the cast continued to work hard, making progress primarily because two of them stood in as understudies for Sprite and Feathering. Yet the total company, including Fransk, became increasingly frustrated, a frustration that grew as the pressure of opening night drew closer.

Finally, on Tuesday morning, the eleventh scheduled day of rehearsal, Sprite and Feathering told Fransk they would be at rehearsal again beginning that night. Both, while still sick, were well enough to work and perform.

Fransk anticipated Tuesday's rehearsal with eagerness, as did the entire cast. As rehearsal progressed, however, it became apparent that Sprite and Feathering knew neither their lines nor their blocking. In fact, it seemed to Fransk that neither of them had worked on the play at all. They looked and sounded as if they were seeing the script for the first time. Fransk felt betrayed. Cast morale plummeted. Throughout the rehearsal Fransk said nothing.

After quietly dismissing the cast and announcing that Wednesday's rehearsal would begin a half hour earlier than usual, he sat down with Jamison to discuss the problem.

Questions

1. What problems, if any, does this case present?

2. At what points, if any, might Fransk have avoided the problems?

3. Analyze the options available to Fransk in his handling of Sprite and Feathering.

4. What should Fransk do?

CASE 27. LAST-MINUTE CHANGES: *WHERE HAS TOMMY FLOWERS GONE?* (B)

Richard Fransk returned to his office. It was Christmastime and he had just passed John Sprite and Martha Feathering, talking in the theatre greenroom with several other cast members from *Where Has Tommy Flowers Gone?* Almost four months had passed since the summer repertory production had closed in early August. Yet the cast was still defending his action to the disgruntled acting pair. He wondered once again whether or not he had made a correct decision.

Review of Fransk's action

On that Tuesday night in July, Fransk had talked with Jamison about his possibilities. Sprite and Feathering had not only missed a week of rehearsal, they had promised to work on the play by themselves, and then had betrayed that promise. Continuing as if nothing unusual had happened seemed impossible. Fransk felt devastated, and he was sure that the continued presence of Sprite and Feathering would have a detrimental effect on the rest of the cast. Even if they somehow "pulled it off" in performance, Fransk thought, his own integrity and his responsibility to everybody else demanded some kind of action. Consequently, at midnight he called the two at home. Feathering answered the phone.

"I've decided to make a change," Fransk explained. "I trusted you and you let me down. So I'm going to recast the role of Netta. You will no longer be in the play."

"I'm sorry you feel that way because I really wanted to be in the play," responded Feathering. "It was my one chance to play a really good role. But I guess I understand, and I'm sorry I got sick. Good luck with it. Do you want to talk to John?"

Fransk talked with Sprite, explaining that the role of Tommy would also be recast. Both conversations were civil, without regrets or hysteria.

Within an hour Fransk had called the two actors who had stood in during Sprite and Feathering's absences, asking if they would play Tommy and Netta. Both agreed to accept the new roles. They also agreed not to say anything to anyone else about the change and to come to an early 4 p.m. rehearsal the next day. Then Fransk and Jamison began to alter the script. By dawn, though Fransk knew it would diminish the play's effectiveness, they had rewritten the entire script in substantial ways, eliminating completely the two now vacant roles. while editing the roles of Tommy and Netta by cutting almost one-third of their respective lines.

Fransk rehearsed with the new lead cast members from 4 to 6 p.m. on Wednesday afternoon, then met with the company. His announcement that Sprite and Feathering had been replaced was greeted with obvious joy. Cast morale rose instantly. He also announced that Tommy and Netta would rehearse from 4 to 6:30 and 10 to 12 each day before opening, that the two remaining regular evening rehearsals for the total cast needed to be completely productive, and that Friday's opening night had been changed from a performance to a final open dress rehearsal. The cast, gripped by the energy that often accompanies crisis, surged through rehearsal as never before, working with renewed dedication and purpose.

Friday night *Where Has Tommy Flowers Gone?* was ready for a dress rehearsal, although Tommy and Netta were still on book for about half the play. Fransk announced to the small opening night audience (approximately 100 people) that they were seeing a dress rehearsal rather than a performance because of last-minute cast changes necessitated by illness. Some actors, he told them, would be holding scripts. Consequently, the evening would be free of admission charge; those with tickets purchased earlier could get their refund at intermission. He also encouraged those who wished to leave; they could return for a performance in the following weeks. (Only a small handful of the audience left.)

In the week that followed Fransk continued rehearsals with the cast, and by the second performance, the following Friday, he thought *Where Has Tommy Flowers Gone?* was completely presentable. It was not, to be sure, a strong production, but it was rehearsed and performed by a cast that felt good about the changes he had made and who had pulled together as best they could.

Question

1. Analyze Fransk's decisions and his methods for carrying them out.

Chapter V   Working with Other Collaborators

CASE 28. THE SET DESIGNER: *THE HOUSE OF BLUE LEAVES*

The Open Hearth Dinner Theatre had been running success-fully for eight years, during which time its reputation for outstanding food and theatre had become well established.

Founded by Peter Duffield, the operation had grown over the years to include two full-time directors, a technical director, a costumer, a lighting designer and an adequate staff for food service, administration and technical production. Each year, though, Duffield hired a different visiting artist to design scenery. In this way, he thought, theatre patrons could enjoy changing visual emphasis for the plays presented, and the theatre itself would not fall into undesirable repetition in scenic style. The idea had worked well, and the theatre had been able to attract outstanding young professional designers from throughout the country.

The theatre produced fifteen plays a year with a resident, professional acting company. Each play ran seven perfor-mances a week for three weeks. The two directors alternated productions, a system that permitted three weeks of directo-rial preparation and three weeks of rehearsal for each play.

The eleventh play scheduled during one season in the early 1980's was John Guare's *The House of Blue Leaves,* a serious comedy that staff director Linda Smith had wanted to direct for some time. In fact, her ideas for the production had been developing for two years, and she looked forward with eager anticipation to seeing them fulfilled. Rehearsals were to begin in less than a week.

Smith had tried on several occasions to talk with visiting designer Dennis Crane about the production, but each time he had been called away to solve some more immediate problem. Crane, Smith thought, had been only partially effective throughout the year. Though his designs were workmanlike, she thought they lacked imagination and flair. She had also found him temperamental and fairly uncommu-nicative. Shy and reserved, he had remained aloof from the rest of the company.

When Crane canceled still another design conference just three days before rehearsals were scheduled to begin, Smith mentioned her concerns to Duffield as he was leaving for two weeks in New York to audition actors for the following season. He told her he would be sure before he left that Crane kept the next morning free.

Smith and Crane met at 10 a.m. the next day to talk about *The House of Blue Leaves* for the first time. After the usual amenities and before she could talk about the play at all, Crane said to her, "You know, I haven't read the play yet, partly because there just hasn't been time. And I don't know much about it. But I've got a design concept that I think should be exciting for it. You'll like it. I'll get it drawn tonight and show you tomorrow." Before she could respond, Crane had to leave for another meeting.

Question

1. What should Smith do?

CASE 29. THE LIGHTING DESIGNER: *OEDIPUS REX*

Richard Alman (director), Betty Jones (lighting designer) and Bruce Garrett (technical director) sat down together to set lighting cues two days before the first full technical rehearsal for *Oedipus Rex*. The stage manager, Jeanne Robbins, joined them. Alman and Jones had worked closely together for a month, and Alman had approved the overall lighting design some days earlier. Now the instruments were hung and focused, the circuiting had been completed, and the time had come to program into the computer all the specific cues for the production.

Questions

1. What is Alman's role at this moment? What is Jones's role?

2. How do you work best with a lighting designer?

CASE 30. THE PLAYWRIGHT: *ECLIPSE OF THE MOON*

Nan Deeter had been contracted as a visiting artist to direct the world premier of *Eclipse of the Moon* at the Washington Repertory Theatre (WRT), a regional professional theatre in Seattle, and she did not know the playwright, Sheila Harris, who would also be a visiting artist-in-residence throughout the entire production period. The WRT flew them both to the Northwest one month before auditions to meet each other.

Deeter was eager to explore the parameters which would govern the relationship between director and playwright for *Eclipse;* to do this, she knew, she would have to be able to articulate her own most effective way of working with a playwright. Indeed, Harris had written to her, saying, in part, "I'm eager to hear how you want to work together. I know the script needs real attention, and I hope we can improve it as rehearsals progress."

Now Deeter began to think of her coming conversation with Harris.

Questions

1. What kind of things should Deeter be prepared to discuss at her meeting with Harris?

2. What's important to you, as a director, when you work with a playwright on a new script?

CASE 31. THE DESIGN TEAM: *KASPAR*

Director Elinor Watkins looked at the list she held in her hands:

Alan Crow	Set Designer
Michael Smith	Lighting Designer
Karen Lamb	Costume Designer
Tom Foigne	Property Designer
Michelle Founder	Sound Designer
Leslie Combs	Stage Manager

These were the people scheduled to meet with her the next day for what Combs had described as the "first design meeting" for the Red River University Theatre production of Peter Handke's *Kaspar.* A visiting director from another university halfway across the state, Watkins had met none of her future collaborators, but she knew that some were students, some were faculty. She also knew that Lamb and Crow had only minimal design experience.

As she reviewed the list before her, Watkins began to plan for the meeting.

Background

An experienced director who worked regularly off Broadway in addition to her university responsibilities, Watkins also frequently served as guest artist for other campus theatres. *Kaspar,* however, would be her first experience at Red River, where the theatre program was strong and active. A mid-sized, comprehensive institution that offered both the B.F.A. and M.F.A. in Theatre, Red River employed seven full-time faculty who worked with almost 150 theatre students, all but a handful of whom were undergraduates. An active production program featured nine mainstage plays each year, and often as many as a hundred other productions, which ranged from single performances of one-acts to open-ended runs of full-length pieces. Strongly focused on education, the faculty tried earnestly to get students involved in major production assignments as soon as they seemed prepared. Faculty also tried to insure that students and faculty worked together as colleagues whenever possible.

As a result, the Red River program had earned a deserved-
ly fine reputation that attracted outstanding students in all
areas of theatre and prepared them primarily for entry-level
positions in the professional theatre. Students were nurtured carefully through learning experiences, all the while
being encouraged to assume greater and greater responsibilities.

Alan Crow was perhaps a typical example. A junior design
major, he had begun in his first year with a course in
stagecraft, had then progressed through Drafting I and II into
Concepts of Design and, finally, into Scene Design. Along the
way, in addition to his classroom and laboratory assignments,
he had designed settings for two one-act plays directed by
graduate students, had served as the assistant set designer for
one mainstage production, and had helped draft working
drawings for seven different faculty and student designers.
Everyone agreed he was now ready for *Kaspar,* which would
be his first major design assignment.

The design meeting

Watkins was pleased to be directing at Red River, and with
auditions still a month away, she knew there was time to work
effectively with the various designers before the hectic pace
of rehearsals began. She had worked with many designers
over the years, but she knew that working with new designers
for the first time presented special challenges.

As she held the list of her future collaborators, Watkins
began to review what she would say to them at the first
scheduled meeting, now less than twenty-four hours away.
Mostly, she knew, she would try to let them know about her
own expectations concerning the design process. She had
even prepared a one-page statement to give them, which she
hoped would serve as a stimulus for initial conversation. That
statement included nine specific comments and had a fairly
direct title.

What I Want from Designers

1. We'll talk about it a lot, I hope, and explore your ideas
as well as mine, but what I want at the end of this talk is

eventual agreement about the play itself. We must all end up working on the same production of this very complex piece.

2. I want to pursue ideas with you as they come along, not just be given ideas once they have fully bloomed.

3. I want to have many—or at least several—ideas to choose among. Multiple options are important to me because I think every problem has more than one possible solution.

4. I want you to have a concern for actors in everything we do.

5. I want you to be realistic about time schedules. When you tell me something can be done by such-and-such a date, I will believe you—and I will expect it to be done by then.

6. I also want you to be realistic about budget and about all the other resources available to us.

7. I want you to pay attention to detail.

8. I want you to work, first, with little drawings and notes and scribbles on the backs of envelopes and scrap paper, not with full-blown, time-consuming renderings or plots or whatever. (This related directly to no. 2 above.)

9. I want you to know how to do things, to get things accomplished. In other words, I will assume you know well the tools, materials, techniques and whatnot of design and fulfillment of that design.

Watkins felt pleased with her list, even though she knew it was but a beginning. She also knew that designers, too, were individuals, each with a unique way of working best. What would these particular designers want from her, she wondered?

Questions

1. Analyze Watkins's list. What are its strengths and weaknesses? What does it say about her as a director?

2. What would you advise Watkins to add to her list at this point?

3. What would you advise Watkins about her first meeting with the designers for *Kaspar?*

4. How do you work best with designers in these very early stages of production? What questions do you hope they will ask?

CASE 32. THE DIRECTING TEAM:
SPOON RIVER ANTHOLOGY

Alvin Cohen began to think about his next job. A successful freelance director, Cohen had just signed a contract to direct a touring production of *Spoon River Anthology* for the Island Theatre, a large regional professional theatre that, in addition to its main subscription season and an alternative season of experimental plays, also mounted four touring productions each year. *Spoon River Anthology,* after it played eight performances on the Island Theatre stage, had been booked for forty-two performances in two months at high schools and community centers throughout the state.

Cohen knew that the massive resources of Island Theatre would be available for his use. He also knew that this directing job was not one he would do alone. Alan Diner, the Island Theatre Administrative Director, had told him he would be assigned the obvious artistic collaborators for the production, people to serve as scenic, lighting, costume and property designers. There would also be the supporting administrative staff—those who managed audiences, ticket sales, publicity and marketing. More importantly, said Diner, there would be those who would work directly with Cohen as part of a "directing team." Diner said Cohen would enjoy the collaboration of

a stage manager
an assistant stage manager
a production stage manager
a road manager
a company manager
a casting assistant
a musical director
a choreographer
an assistant director
a dramaturg
an acting coach
a voice coach
a movement coach
a dialect coach, if needed

a fight director, if needed
others, as needed.

In working with this team, Diner said, Cohen should strive to insure his overall vision for the production while also freeing the creativity of every other participant.

Questions

1. How can Cohen best work with each of these members of the direction team? What advice would you give him?

2. How would you define the responsibility for each of these positions?

3. What other members of a directing team might a director find helpful at times?

CASE 33. THE STAGE MANAGER: *THE BEGINNER*

Julie Colthorn had been invited to Wessimenn College as a guest director for the production of a new script titled *The Beginner*. Plans called for her to visit the campus for three days in November for preliminary meetings and design conferences, to visit again in December for three days for further preliminary work, then to return in January for auditions and six weeks of rehearsal before opening night. *The Beginner* was scheduled for seven performances, Tuesday through Sunday evenings, with a matinee on Saturday.

In November, no sooner had Colthorn arrived on campus than a sophomore theatre major came to her saying, "I'm Robert Pine, and I would like very much to be the stage manager for *The Beginner*." Colthorn had been told by the director of theatre that Pine would approach her, and that he might make a good stage manager; he'd never done this job before, but he had acted in one or two productions, seemed organized and efficient, and wanted to work on this new script with a new director.

Colthorn and Pine talked awhile, then she scheduled a meeting with him for December, at which time they agreed to explore in some detail her expectations for a stage manager.

When they met in December, Colthorn reviewed with Pine a brief worksheet she had compiled.

The Beginning List
A Stage Manager's Job

Pre-Audition
  Coordinate master calendar
  Prepare call-board
  Schedule audition notices
  Begin prompt book
During Auditions
  Greet actors
  Distribute audition forms
  Collect résumés
  Distribute and collect scripts
  Keep timed lists of arrivals
During Rehearsals
  Tape ground plan on rehearsal floor

142

Distribute rehearsal schedules
Set up rehearsal space nightly
Clean rehearsal space (before and after rehearsal)
Maintain prompt board
Take blocking notes
Be ready to prompt
Note all cues: lights, sound, props, etc.
Maintain call-board
During Dress Rehearsals
Be the primary coordinator
Treat rehearsals as performances
Set up rehearsal equipment
Call all cues
Scenery shifts
Prepare and post sign-in sheets
Check with actors daily about their needs
Keep rehearsal log
During Performances
Make a "Things to Do" list
Time performances
Coordinate with house manager
Spike set
Check props
Check lights
Call cast, beginning at ½ hour before curtain
Post reviews and other items
After Closing
We'll discuss this
Always
Be aware of safety
Remember: the cast comes first
Keep track of needed repairs

Colthorn discussed each item individually with Pine, and he seemed to understand her overall sense of the job. To her mind, however, it was more important that Pine understand her second list, which she had titled "Dos and Don'ts for Stage Managers: An Attitudinal Profile of Fifty-one Selected Items of Equal Importance in Random Order":

1. Never invoke the name of the director.
2. Never tell or order anyone to do anything. Always ask.
3. Never ask anyone to do anything you can do yourself.

4. Be totally mature.
5. Strive for low visibility. (Invisibility is best.)
6. Be still. (Do not speak unnecessarily. Ever.)
7. Be sure.
8. Stay close to the director.
9. Do things unobtrusively. (No one should know anything is being done.)
10. Use your feet first.
11. Answer only factual questions.
12. Double-check everything. (Twice.)
13. Keep lists. (Use them.)
14. Never appear rushed.
15. Never appear harassed.
16. Never appear out of control.
17. Never speak loudly. (Never raise your voice.)
18. Speak quietly. (Always.)
19. Listen. (Carefully.)
20. Watch. (Carefully.)
21. Be supportive of the production and its people in every way.
22. Treat everyone exactly the same.
23. Remember, stage managers never "take five."
24. Anticipate.
25. Have it done before it's needed.
26. Have it done before someone asks for it to be done.
27. Maintain total and absolute discretion. (Without exception.)
28. Know who knows.
29. Praise strength.
30. Overlook weakness.
31. Never hurry.
32. Be scrupulously organized.
33. Assume responsibility. (Don't wait for it to be assigned.)
34. Never become emotionally involved.
35. Talk only to your canary.
36. Do not attempt to resolve the problems of others.
37. Do not direct.
38. Do not design.
39. Do not act.
40. Eliminate your own ego.
41. Watch for actor comfort.
42. Maintain an even temperament.
43. Avoid all conflicts.
44. Lead by example.
45. Be clear.

46. Remember: to exert authority is to lose it.
47. Remain calm.
48. Be error free.
49. Be sure everything runs smoothly all the time.
50. Think.
51. Ask questions.

The stage manager's worksheet was important, Colthorn thought, but the "Attitudinal Profile" was even more so. It defined, for her, not just what she expected a stage manager to accomplish, but also the manner and style in which that accomplishment should occur.

Questions

1. Analyze Colthorn's brief worksheet. What would you advise Colthorn to add to it or delete from it?

2. Analyze Colthorn's "Attitudinal Profile."

3. What are the qualities you, as a director, find most desirable in a stage manager? Are they the same as or different from the qualities Colthorn desires?

CASE 34. THE TECHNICAL CREW:
SHE STOOPS TO CONQUER

The two-person theatre staff at Silver College had never gotten along very well together. Director Barry Michaels and designer/technical director George Baldwin just didn't agree with each other very often—about anything. Nevertheless, both were charismatic, talented men, and in spite of obvious friction that had created separate and often hostile student factions, they had worked together as co-equals for three years to produce some outstanding theatre for their small, rural college community.

Their differences had been especially severe during the production of Oliver Goldsmith's *She Stoops to Conquer.* Michaels had suggested the play, but Baldwin had argued against it, giving his reluctant approval only after long and often bitter discussion. Then, having accepted the play, Baldwin had wanted to design and build an authentic eighteenth-century production, primarily to give students experience in historical theatre technique. "If we're going to do a period play," he said, "then let's really do a period play." But Michaels had envisioned a contemporary production in modern dress, to let students know, once again, that classic plays need to be reinterpreted for every age. "I'm not interested in museum theatre," he told Baldwin. Eventually, the two men had compromised on a late-nineteenth-century production, a solution neither of them found entirely satisfactory. Resolving their differences had consumed almost two weeks of what had been scheduled as production time.

The shortened production period meant Baldwin soon fell helplessly behind in preparing the set, costumes and furniture. Though his fifteen or so committed technical theatre students worked all night long, night after night, to complete the necessary construction, the first technical rehearsal arrived with the set only half finished, with lights hung and cabled, but still unfocused, and with costumes ready only for a first fitting. And the entire crew was exhausted.

Meanwhile, Michaels had also felt the pressure of inadequate time. His actors were having unusual difficulty with the unfamiliar language and they had somehow failed to capture

a style of performance that could reveal the rich humor of Goldsmith's script. Michaels, as was his habit, held himself responsible for the shortcomings, but couldn't seem to discover any means to bring the play to life. Like the cast's, his discouragement had grown deep.

In the midst of fatigue, anger and discouragement, students and faculty prepared for the first technical rehearsal, scheduled for 7 p.m. five days before opening night. Michaels arrived at the theatre an hour early with the acting company, to have a line rehearsal, and discovered the crew painting the floor. It would not, he knew, be dry by the scheduled curtain time. In a moment of frustration, he lashed out angrily at the students working on stage. Baldwin heard the outburst from the light booth where he was writing cues. He called all his crew members together, talked with them a few minutes on stage, then with them stalked out of the theatre.

Question

1. What should Michaels do?

Chapter VI   Special Problems in Directing

CASE 35. THEATRE SAFETY:
SURVIVAL RESEARCH LABORATORY

The Survival Research Laboratory (SRL) is a performance group from San Francisco. Their futuristic, bombastic choreography defies adequate definition within the normal confines of traditional theatre.

Founded in the late 1970's by designer and engineer Mark Pauline, the SRL presents open-air extravaganzas created by large-scale machines propelled by robot technology. These manufactured, mechanical giants carry names like the "Shock-Wave Cannon," which with its sound blast can shatter glass from a hundred yards away; the flame-throwing "Sprinkler from Hell," which literally throws flames—as if it were some post-industrial dragon—-more than fifty yards out from its black metal mouth; and the "Walking Machine with Flamethrower," a spindly-legged smaller fire belcher whose movement and activity are determined randomly by a guinea pig playing in a cage. The machines are controlled, except for the guinea pig, by human manipulators using radio transmitters, fully visible to the audience. They follow their monsters as if riding in a wake of safety. As Cathy Ragland, a critic for the *Seattle Weekly,* has written, these "automated creatures plunge, hurdle, and explode into one another amid blending sparks of electricity, bursts of fire, and the raging sonic flourishes of an equally disturbing sound track. It's like an industrial vaudeville show . . . that lurks somewhere between art and technology." The machines, like knights of old, battle each other to death. The remains, charred and burned, end their slow-motion dances in total destruction, and come to rest in the performance space as if they were bodies on a battleground.

SRL performances take place outside, in abandoned lots and deserted yards. A 1990 performance in Seattle took place in a large railroad lot, roughly the size of a football field, south of the landmark Kingdome. Titled *Carnival of Misplaced Direction: Calculated to Arouse Resentment for the Principles of Order,* the piece marked SRL's second appearance in this Puget Sound city.

There is excitement in a SRL performance. There is also danger. Electricity, fire, smoke and sound combine with the lumbering movement of metal dinosaurs to engage the audience in a spectacle more brutal than NFL football on a Sunday afternoon. In fact, the danger—and the potential danger—is so real that audience members for the Seattle performance on June 23, 1990, were required to sign a release before they were admitted to the performance area.

This is an important legal document;
please read carefully before signing.

AGREEMENT NOT TO SUE

I am aware that, during the performance of Survival Research Laboratories (SRL), certain dangers may arise, including but not limited to deafening noises, unanticipated surprises and changes in circumstances that may terrify and upset me, propellants from the machines in the performance or from the pyrotechnical activity, the activities of other attendants, the condition of terrain on which the scaffolding is constructed, and the collapse of scaffolding.

In consideration of the right to attend the SRL performance, I have and do assume all of the risks (whether caused by negligence or not) inherent in attending this performance or similar performances, including without limitation those risks specifically set out in the preceding paragraph. I also agree to hold harmless and release the City of Seattle, the Center on Contemporary Art, SRL and all sponsoring persons and entities (public and private, corporate and noncorporate) from any and all liability, action, causes of action, debts, claims, demands of every kind and nature whatsoever which may arise out of or in connection with my attendance of the SRL performance, to the full extent allowed under applicable law. In simple terms this means that I WILL NOT SUE THE CITY OF SEATTLE, THE CENTER ON CONTEMPORARY ART, SRL, OR ANYONE OR ANYTHING ELSE WITH RESPECT TO THE SRL PERFORMANCE.

The terms of this instrument shall serve as a release and assumption of risk for my heirs, executor and administrator and all members of my family, including any minors accompanying me.

I certify that I am over eighteen years of age and legally competent to sign this instrument; that I understand that the terms of this instrument are contractual and not mere recitals; that I have read and do understand this agreement not to sue and that I have signed this instrument of my own free will. I also understand that, if I do not wish to sign this agreement not to sue, the purchase price of my ticket will be refunded.

I have been informed that *earplugs* or other devices to protect one's hearing *are strongly recommended* and can be purchased at the site of the performance.

DATED June ____ , 1990.

Name _____
      Please Print
Signed _____
Parent or Gardian [*sic*] _____
           If under 18

An audience of 3,000 waited, as if for a rock concert, almost three hours on a hot Seattle night before the chain link fence opened to permit entrance to the performance area. Once in the railroad yard, they passed stands where earplugs sold for a dollar a pair, then searched for viewing space. Some sat on the ground or found places on the specially erected stadium bleachers; some found their way to the roofs of neighboring buildings; some climbed to stand at the top of temporary wooden scaffolding; still others hung over a nearby bridge, and stayed there even after a loudspeaker warning about fire and electrical sparks. In all, spectators surrounded three-quarters of the performance field, with only a smattering of people on the fourth side, which was obviously designed as "backstage" space.

During the performance, flamethrowers frequently forced the audience in a huddled mass to back up some twenty yards or more, smoke fully enveloped whole spectator sections several times, a full-scale building burned to the ground as sparks flew in the wind, and the massive machines—as planned—searched for one another's weaknesses in a choreography of violence, eventually destroying one another in an unsettling war of technological confrontation, accompanied all the while by ear-splitting sounds caused by the machines themselves, reinforced by an equally loud sound track which blared from ample speakers.

When the devastation was complete and the twisted metal at last fell silent, the audience departed, leaving behind a smoldering contemporary battlefield.

Questions

1. Analyze the SRL's "Agreement Not to Sue." Of what value is it? (You may want to consult an attorney on this one.)

2. Would you, as an audience member, sign such a release?

3. As a director, under what other circumstances might you ask audience members to sign a pre-performance agreement? Under what circumstances might you warn audience members in some other way? How?

4. What role should the audience safety play in the planning of a performance?

CASE 36. THE LARGE CAST: *INHERIT THE WIND*

The Pinero Community College production of Lawrence and Lee's *Inherit the Wind* closed after its five evening performances, and director James R. Wiley was supervising a successful strike, which was attended by all fifty-nine cast members, in addition to the relatively large crew. As he watched the cast move around the dismantled set like ants disturbed in their nest, Wiley thought back to the rehearsals and performances of the production. He was young (twenty-six years old), and while he had directed ten productions during his graduate study and in his three years at Pinero, never before had he worked with a cast of more than seven actors. Therefore, the fifty-nine actors in *Inherit the Wind*—lawyers, witnesses, preachers, townspeople, reporters, spectators, jury members—at times had overwhelmed him. The sheer number of bodies, the slow pace of progress, the logistical nightmares, the painful coordination of schedules, the communication hurdles—these and other concerns had often conspired against him as he worked to get the production ready for performance.

Soon there would be time to reflect, to see if "next time" he might be able to proceed with greater smoothness, increased effectiveness and stronger confidence. In fact, as the strike finished, he began to organize his thoughts so that he could deal with the various issues before they slipped out of his mind.

He had come to believe that the concerns of dealing with a large cast were fundamentally different from the concerns of dealing with a small cast. For one thing, obviously, they affected many more people. Yet he also thought that such concerns could be anticipated, examined and, perhaps, even resolved without disruption to the process of rehearsal and production, but only if he dealt with them now.

When he finally got home at the end of the evening, he sat down with paper and pencil to write the following questions:

1. What factors should influence choosing to direct a play that has a large cast? (Wiley had wanted to involve many people in the theatre program, and to that end had decided Pinero should present at least two large-cast plays each year.)

2. How should auditions for a large-cast play be managed? (Wiley remembered that more than two hundred hopeful students had auditioned for *Inherit the Wind*.)

3. Is there a way to encourage those not cast to participate in some other way in the production? (Wiley hoped, especially, he could keep the interest of these people so they might audition again.)

4. What should happen at the first rehearsal? (Wiley remembered meeting the almost sixty cast members for the first time. He didn't know them. They didn't know him. Most of them didn't know one another. None of them knew the play. Fewer than half had ever acted before.)

5. How can rehearsals best be planned? (Wiley remembered the time involved in dealing with so many people, and the sheer logistics of determining who should be where, when.)

6. How does a large cast affect blocking? (If Wiley had learned anything at all it was that moving fifty people on stage was different from moving two people.)

7. What might be the best way to give notes to a large cast? (Whether in the early blocking rehearsals or in the final dress rehearsals, Wiley found that his communication with the cast was influenced by the number of people involved. When he wanted to work for a while with an individual actor, for example, he never quite knew what to do with all the others. Often they ended up just standing around, waiting. Some, he recalled, waited less patiently than others.)

8. How does a large cast affect other theatre artists? The costumer, for example? (Costumes for *Inherit the Wind* had been designed by a student costumer; there were some actors she had apparently not seen at all until the first dress rehearsal.)

9. How does a large cast change things like focus, rhythm, pace, picturization and all of the other elements in a director's work?

10. How does a large cast influence the work of a stage manager? (For one thing, Wiley thought, having just one assistant stage manager was not enough.)

11. What are the best ways to use cast members in rehearsal? (Wiley wanted to think especially about how often

various cast members should be called for rehearsal. Surely, he thought, the hot dog seller should work less than the primary lawyer; where, he wondered, could he find the dividing line between "not enough" and "too much"?)

12. Is there an effective way to organize backstage activity? (Wiley found that during dress rehearsals, for example, fifty-nine people overwhelmed the make-up room and the dressing rooms.)

Wiley knew there were other questions which also needed to be addressed.

Questions

1. Is Wiley's assumption correct? Are there directorial differences between a large- and a small-cast production?

2. What specific advice would you give Wiley about each of his questions?

3. What further questions would you add to his list?

CASE 37. REVIVAL: *DR. FAUSTUS*

The Milenberg University Theatre produced Christopher Marlowe's *Dr. Faustus* early in March 1985. The production opened in the ninety-eight-seat Fair Hall Theatre after a four-week rehearsal period during which the cast worked three or more hours a day, six days a week. All fifty-four actors in the company were undergraduate students at the small, church-related, liberal arts college, as were the twenty-eight additional crew members, and only a few had any previous theatre experience. Twenty of the actors, in fact, were freshmen.

In spite of youth and inexperience, the production proved a major success with critics and audiences alike. Director Larry Mill "created sheer theatrical magic," one reviewer wrote, "maneuvering more than fifty actors on the postage-stamp stage as if he had all of Saxony in his control." Another critic explained, "Even though we have become accustomed at Milenberg to excellent productions and high quality acting, *Dr. Faustus,* far surpasses the usual standard. Overall, it may well be the best college theatre production I've seen in recent years." Audiences evidently concurred with this critical judgment, for all eight performances sold out.

A day or two after the opening, Professor Mill was invited to repeat the play for two special performances during Parents' Weekend in May. The revival would involve moving the production from Fair Hall to the Milenberg Field House, so that as many as eighteen hundred persons could see each performance. The massive annual influx of parents, alumni and friends would virtually assure sellout houses both nights.

Mill asked the cast and crew what they thought about the possibility. Eager for the additional experience and excited by the potential for a larger audience, they all agreed their individual schedules could be arranged to make further rehearsal and performance possible.

When, after further thought, Mill announced a positive decision backstage on closing night, the company cheered. After strike, during which scenery, properties and costumes were carefully stored for later use, Mill gathered the company together, urged them to keep the play fresh in their minds, then announced he would contact them in April with plans for the revival.

On April 21 he sent the entire company—cast and crews—the following letter:

> To the *Dr. Faustus* Company:
>
> Here we go again!
>
> Congratulations on eight good performances. Now our objective for May 7 and 8 is two even better ones. You're on the spot a lot worse than if you had fallen on your faces last March. Let the word get out that we have a hit on our hands, and up go the expectations of all who haven't seen it yet. Plus, the ones who will be seeing it for the second time—yes, there will be many—will have only a faded memory of something brilliant in the past.
>
> Our first rehearsal will be Sunday, May 2, in the Field House at 6:45 p.m. Total cast and crew. (Crews will be released after the week's plans are laid.)
>
> On Monday and Tuesday, May 3 and 4, we will have short unit rehearsals of individual scenes. Let me know soon if there are times or days you would prefer not to rehearse so I can try to arrange the schedule accordingly.
>
> On Wednesday night, May 5, we'll have a run-through.
>
> On Thursday night, May 6, we'll have a dress rehearsal.
>
> Then, Friday and Saturday, May 7 and 8: PERFORMANCES.
>
> *Please* don't make me regret the long "vacation" by dropping lines at our Sunday rehearsal. Review your role—and the entire play—frequently between now and then. Fair Hall is always open if you wish to walk through the play by yourself or with somebody.
>
> Also, begin to strengthen your voices. The Field House—in case you hadn't noticed—requires a bit more projection than Fair!
>
> You should also begin to think about what differences the new space will mean for movement and blocking. Remember, our stage will be three times bigger than before.
>
> On Saturday afternoon, May 1, we'll be moving sets, props, costumes, etc., to the Field House via truck and

car; feel free to come and help if you have the time and inclination. The more, the merrier—also the faster. We'll start at 2:00.

Finally, let me say how much I look forward to doing this play again. It has been a pet theory of mine that if a cast could sit on a production for a couple of months and then return to it, good things could result. Prove me right!

In the week after he sent the letter, Professor Mill began to review just what the revival of *Dr. Faustus* would actually entail. He wondered what problems, if any, he should anticipate, and how he could avoid or solve them. He also wanted to analyze carefully his planned rehearsal schedule, to be sure that five rehearsal evenings would be sufficient for remounting the production.

Questions

1. What problems, if any, should Mill anticipate?

2. How should he solve or avoid these problems?

3. Analyze Mills rehearsal schedule for May 2–6.

CASE 38. OUTDOOR THEATRE: AELSEP ARTS FAIR

The Outdoor Arts Fair in Aelsep, Minnesota was a week-long festival of informal arts events presented throughout the city each year in late April. Begun in 1983 and funded primarily by the city government, the fair provided short performances staged throughout the city in twelve different locations over a five-day period. In eleven of the locations, events were staged daily at noon and 4 p.m. In Elwood Park, a highly traveled "green space" located near downtown, performances occurred throughout the day at unannounced times.

John Lee Brighton, a director for the Aelsep Community Theatre (ACT), had been invited to direct for the 1986 Arts Fair. The news director for a local television station, Brighton shared directing responsibilities at ACT with four other volunteer directors, and he was considered a capable theatre person. In fact, during his seven-year affiliation with ACT, the group had grown considerably, both in quality and in level of community support. Participation in the Outdoors Arts Fair, however, would provide the theatre's first experience outside its own building, a converted railroad station with excellent performance and support space.

After careful consideration, Brighton had chosen to direct three short story-theatre pieces, two of which he had already selected. (These plays can be found in Appendices I and II of this case.) The three plays would be performed as a single unit, perhaps a half-hour long, with a single company of actors. While almost a month remained before auditions in March, Brighton, who was accustomed to directing only in ACT's intimate proscenium theatre, had already begun to consider the problems he might face working out-of-doors in an informal environment. Instinct told him the differences might somehow be significant, so he had drawn up a beginning list of questions for himself:

1. Will there be distractions outside and what should I do about them?
2. How will the audience be arranged?
3. Do I need to worry about attracting attention and gathering an audience at the beginning of each performance?

4. What will happen to focus?

5. How can I insure that audience members can see and hear?

6. Should the plays have an elastic beginning? How should the performance end?

7. In what ways should movement styles and patterns differ from productions of the same plays performed indoors?

8. Will these particular performance pieces be effective out-of-doors? Why?

9. Will I need any equipment and/or technical support? Why? How should I handle this support, if it is necessary?

10. What happens if it rains?

11. How can I prepare the cast for performing outdoors?

12. Should I use music in the production? If so, how?

As Brighton perused his questions, he knew that further concerns should be added to the list. He also realized that his attention seemed focused on four general areas: the nature of outdoor informal performance; the anticipation of outdoor audience behavior; the process of rehearsal and preparation for performing outdoors; and play selection for the outdoor environment. In each of these and other areas, he knew, decisions would have to be made before rehearsals began.

Brighton's most immediate problem, however, was to decide just where the plays should be performed. Nancy Darian, an employee of Aelsep's Parks and Recreation Department and coordinator for the festival, had offered him two choices. He could use the wide, sweeping steps of the Aelsep Court House, or any of the spaces in Elwood Park. As Brighton thought back to his earlier visits to these spaces, he realized anew the significant difference between the two. As Darian had explained, the Court House would offer a seated audience, a scheduled performance time and an almost formal amphitheatre setting. Elwood Park, on the other hand, regardless of the exact locations he might choose, would provide considerable pedestrian traffic, wide-open space, no defined audience area and an unannounced performance time. In neither space, she had explained, could Parks and Recreation provide technical support beyond an adequate sound system and a 20' × 18' open platform, if he should

want either of these items. Brighton had to let Darian know
his preference soon, in order to facilitate her scheduling of
the thirty different events to be presented during the week.

Questions

1. Which performance space option should Brighton
   choose? What differences and problems should he anticipate with each possibility?

2. What additional questions should Brighton add to his
   beginning list?

3. As a consultant to Brighton, how would you advise him on
   each of his questions?

THE TIGER, THE MAN, AND THE MOUSE
adapted by Richard Aumiller

The stage is bare except for a large wooden cage hanging from the ceiling. The raising and lowering of the cage is controlled from off-stage. In general, each character speaks the narration that pertains to himself and acts out the story as he tells it by doing what he says.

TIGER: *(Enters, prowling)* Once upon a time, there was a ferocious tiger *(Growl)* who was very hungry. One evening, he decided to prowl around the jungle and see if he couldn't find someone to eat. He listened very carefully, but he couldn't hear anything. Then he sniffed the air, but he couldn't smell anything. Finally, he looked one way . . . and then, he looked the other way; but he didn't see anything. He was just getting ready to give up and try another part of the jungle, when . . . *(The cage falls over the tiger, who has been backing into position during all of this)* . . . he found himself caught in a trap. He tried to get out through the bars, he tried to ram into the bars, he even tried to chew the bars! But he just couldn't get out.

MAN: *(Enters)* Just then, who should come walking through the jungle but a man, on his way home from working in the fields.

TIGER: When the tiger saw the man, he cried out to him, "Help! I'm trapped in this cage; I can't get out. Please help me. Let me out and I will become your servant. I'll do anything you say; only set me free."

MAN: "Oh no, no! I know what you'd do if I set you free—you'd eat me for supper, that's what you'd do. I'm not going to let you out."

TIGER: *(Sobbing and crying)* "Oh, I could never do that!
                Let me out and I'll prove it; I'll be your friend
                forever. *(The man does not respond; the tiger tries
                a different angle)* Oh, what am I going to do?
                Don't leave me trapped in this cage. They'll
                come and take me far away. They'll put me in a
                circus or a zoo. I'll never see my family again."

MAN: Now the man had begun to cry, too. Men
                cannot stand to see tigers cry. *(The tiger hands
                the man a handkerchief through the bars; the
                man blows his nose very loudly and hands it back)*
                "All right, all right! Since you put it that way,
                I'll let you out." *(The man starts to lift the cage)*

TIGER: But the man had no sooner lifted the cage than
                the tiger leaped out with a mighty roar and
                landed on top of the poor man. "You fool!
                Now what is to prevent me from eating you?
                After being trapped in that cage, I'm hungrier
                than before, I'm so hungry I could eat you in
                one bite." *(The tiger grabs the man's hand and
                prepares to take a big bite; but he is halted by the
                entrance of the mouse)*

MOUSE: *(Entering in a hurry-scurry fashion)* But just as
                the tiger was about to begin his supper, a little
                mouse came scurrying through the jungle.
                When he saw what was about to happen *(The
                mouse stops dead and stares at the tiger and the
                man)*, he shouted out in his loudest squeak:
                "Wait!"

TIGER: "What?"

MOUSE: "Wait!"

TIGER: "Why?"

MOUSE: "Why?"

TIGER: "Why!"

MOUSE: *(Thinking fast)* "Uh . . . I'm confused. I don't understand what's happening here."

MAN: "The tiger here was trapped in the cage there; I set him free and now the ungrateful beast is going to eat me for dinner. It is really quite simple."

MOUSE: *(Acting very flustered)* "Not so simple, not so simple at all! Oh, my poor brain, my poor brain. Now, let me see, let me see; how did it all begin? You *(indicating the man)* were in the cage, and the tiger came walking by . . . ?"

TIGER: "Phooey. What a fool you are, mouse. I was in the cage!"

MOUSE: "Oh, yes, of course, how stupid of me. *(The mouse pretends to tremble in fear)* Yes, I was in the cage—no, I wasn't. Dear, Dear! Where are my wits? Let me see, the tiger was in the man, and the cage came walking by—no, no; that's not it either. I'm afraid you'd better go ahead and finish your dinner. I'm never going to understand."

TIGER: *(In a rage over the mouse's stupidity)* "I'll make you understand. Look here, I'm the tiger . . ."

MOUSE: "Yes, I understand that."

TIGER: "And this is the man . . ."

MOUSE: "Yes, I understand that."

TIGER: "And that is the cage . . ."

MOUSE: "Yes, I understand that."

TIGER: *(Triumphantly)* "And I was in the cage. Do you understand?"

MOUSE: *(Makes a gesture as though he is going to say "yes" again, but at the last moment reconsiders)* "No! Please sir?"

TIGER: *(Impatiently)* "Well?"

MOUSE: "Please sir; how did you get in the cage?"

TIGER: "How? Why in the usual way!"

MOUSE: "Oh, dear me; my head is beginning to spin again. Please don't be angry, but what is the usual way?"

TIGER: *(Jumping into the cage)* "This way, you fool. Now do you understand?"

MOUSE: "Perfectly!" *(He closes the cage over the tiger)* "I understand that you are back to the cage where you belong; and I understand that this is where you will stay this time."

MOUSE   And with that, the Mouse and the Man shook

and   hands and continued on their separate

MAN: ways.

BLACKOUT

MASTER OF ALL MASTERS
adapted by J. Robert Wills from an English folktale

GIRL:	A girl once went to the fair to hire herself for a servant.
MAN:	At last a funny-looking old gentleman hired her, and took her home to his house.
GIRL:	When she got there, he told her that he had something to teach her, for in his house, he had his own name for things. He said to her:
MAN:	What will you call me?
GIRL:	Master or mister, or whatever you please, sir.
MAN:	You must call me "master of all masters." And what would you call this, he said, pointing to the bed.
GIRL:	Bed or couch, or whatever you please, sir.
MAN:	No, that's my barnacle. And what do you call these?
GIRL:	Breeches or trousers or pantaloons, or whatever you please, sir.
MAN:	You must call them squibs and crackers. And what would you call her?
GIRL:	Cat or kitten, or whatever you please, sir.
MAN:	You must call her white-faced simminy. And now, what would you call this?

GIRL: Fire or flame, or whatever you please, sir.

MAN: You must call it hot cockalorum. And what
               this?

GIRL: Water or wet, or whatever you please, sir.

MAN: No, pandalorum is its name. And what do you
               call this?

GIRL: House or cottage, or whatever you please, sir.

MAN: You must call it high topper mountain.

GIRL: And with that, he sent her away and went to
               bed.

MAN: Later that night the servant woke her master
               up in fright.

GIRL: Master of all masters, get out of your barnacle
               and put on your squibs and crackers. For
               white-faced simminy has got a spark of hot
               cockalorum on its tail and unless you get some
               pandalorum, high topper mountain will be all
               hot cockalorum.

CASE 39. INFORMAL THEATRE: EDISON HIGH SCHOOL

Faculty member Oscar Ferranti led the active theatre program at Edison High, a midwestern suburban secondary school with 2,700 students. Even though he and his three theatre faculty colleagues produced four major plays each year, each with an average attendance of about 800 people, Ferranti thought regularly about the vast, untapped potential audience of students, faculty and staff—plus parents, families, friends and other members of Edison's affluent community—whose experience with theatre was less than it should be. Most of them, he reasoned, just didn't know how much fun the theatre could be, or how rewarding; they had never tried it. Because of this, Ferranti had decided that during the next season Edison would not only produce its four regular plays, it would also initiate a series of informal performances, presented, not in the theatre, but wherever the potential audience happened to be. As Ferranti had said to his colleagues, "If people won't come to the theatre, we'll take the theatre to them." Together, students and faculty had decided to concentrate especially in this effort on the potential student audience.

Background

Located in a wealthy suburb northwest of Chicago, not too far from the Wisconsin state line, Edison High drew most of its students from affluent and diverse families. Eighteen percent of its students were African-American; another 21 percent were Asian-American; still another 12 percent were Native American or Hispanic. The remainder were white. This diverse population had thus far escaped in large measure the problems of poverty, drugs and violence which faced most urban secondary schools. Overall, students were highly motivated, enjoyed excellent attendance records, and worked hard in and out of class. Almost 78 percent of the graduating seniors in any given year went on to two-year or four-year colleges or universities.

Over time, the Edison Drama Club had become one of the most popular and prestigious after-school activities. A core of some 120 students worked each year in all phases of theatre production, an endeavor supported by an unusually full curriculum of theatre studies. Students at Edison could take classes in Introduction to the Theatre, Theatre History, Stagecraft, Acting (three semesters), Dance (two semesters), Theatre Design and Independent Study. There was also a Performance Forum, which provided credit for participation in production. Ferranti and his three colleagues taught primarily theatre classes, though each also had other instructional responsibilities—one in English, one in Math, one in Art and one in Music. In addition to directing and producing the four major productions each year—two in the fall, two in the spring—the faculty also supervised two separate evenings of student-directed one-acts.

The plan

Ferranti had talked to both students and faculty about his idea for taking theatre outside the normal theatre space. Everyone expressed enthusiasm, and agreement was soon reached that Ferranti would draw up a plan of possibilities, which would then be discussed at the Edison Drama Club's last meeting of the year. As he had prepared for the meeting, he had decided to write an open memo to faculty and students, in which he would outline some ideas for discussion. The memo was now complete:

> Dear Friends:
>   We've decided to begin next year a series of free, informal performances presented at various times and in various places around the school. The principal will call this "alternative programming"; we'll call it "trying to find an audience while we have fun doing what we want to do."
>   In any case, here are a dozen ideas that might be tried. Many others could—and should—be added to the list of possibilities. The details for each suggestion will have to be worked out, and not all the ideas will work equally well for Edison. But the central idea remains constant: We'll do plays where the people already are, without asking them to go out of their way.

1. *Perform plays on buses while students are on the way to or from school.* Here is a captive audience, often with little to do. Even improvisation in the aisles would be a beginning. Perhaps a different play could be presented on the same bus every day for a week. Or, the same play could "tour" different buses over a period of time. Or, on a given day there could be simultaneous performances on all buses.

2. *Perform plays in the school cafeteria during the lunch hour.* Or, have lunch served in a special place just for those who would like to see a play. An informal version of dinner theatre, lunchtime theatre can also be brown-bag theatre—outside or inside the school building.

3. *Perform plays in the hallways between classes.* See if the crowd can be stopped—or even slowed down—for a few moments of entertainment during a usual "rush hour" of pedestrian traffic.

4. *Perform plays outside in the morning* (or wherever students congregate before school begins). Let audiences start the day with theatre. Students might even be encouraged to arrive early in order to avoid missing any of the play.

5. *Perform plays for non-theatre classes,* as part of the regular academic work of a specific subject. We could volunteer to prepare a play that deals with any subject being studied. Or we could do improvisations based on suggestions from the class. This could work especially well for history, literature or social studies classes. Perhaps the advanced acting class members could do this.

6. *Perform plays at a pep rally.* These would probably need to be specially written, and could even be designed to include audience participation. Perhaps they could also feature the "guest appearance" of a team member or a coach.

7. *Perform plays for those who are waiting in line.* We always seem to generate lines. And what do people do while standing in them? Let them watch a play.

8. *Perform plays for study halls.* In fact, a Study Hall Theatre could be begun—a troupe of actors that could "tour" to different rooms, presenting multiple performances of the same play. Maybe each study hall class could know that once a week (or once a month) they could expect a theatre performance.

9. *Perform plays in the library.* The subject matter and timing could be arranged with the librarian. After all, a library is more than just a place for books.

10. *Perform plays outside after school* (or whenever during the day there are people outside). We could choose a heavy traffic area—a main sidewalk, a natural gathering place, a place near the main exit from the building.

11. *Perform plays during school dances.* What do people do when the band takes a break? Or when the records stop spinning for a while?

12. *Perform plays at the halftime of a football or basketball game.* Why should marching bands have all the fun and attention? Maybe a mime show—or a clown show—could also entertain the crowd while they wait for the second half to begin.

In general, each of these ideas—and many more like them—can let our theatre say to an audience, "Hey! Stop where you are, now, and watch this play," rather than just "Please buy a ticket and come over to the theatre at 8 p.m. next Friday."

The plays we do should be short, probably no longer than ten to twenty minutes, often shorter. They should help create a relaxed atmosphere, free of the formality which often accompanies dramatic presentation. They should be staged in what normally is thought of as non-theatre space. There should be no concern for sets or props or lighting or the other physical aspects of production (except, perhaps, for costuming); plays should be chosen so their success doesn't depend on such technical support.

In addition, the plays should be well rehearsed and excellently performed. The informal atmosphere could lull all of us—directors and actors—into thinking that preparations need not be so diligent for more informal audiences, who will be at least as critical as formal ones, perhaps more so—and holding their attention, when so much else is providing distraction, will be much more difficult.

In any case, I'll look forward to discussing all of these ideas at our meeting.

Questions

1. Analyze Ferranti's list of performance possibilities. Which ones would you advise the Edison Drama Club to accept? To reject? Which possibility would you recommend as "the place to begin"?

2. What possibilities would you add to Ferranti's list? Why?

3. What overall recommendations or warnings would you offer to Ferranti and the Edison Drama Club as they begin this new endeavor?

Note: This case is freely adapted from an article written by J. Robert Wills. Titled "Get 'Em When They Ain't Looking," it appeared in the *Asbestos Curtain* (December 1977).

CASE 40. CENSORSHIP: *NIGHT FIRES*

Night Fires opened off-Broadway at the Jordan Theatre in New York City in April 1988. The play featured review sketches, vaudeville black-outs, musical numbers and short dramatic pieces, a few of which dealt explicitly with gay and lesbian sexual fantasies and realities. This subject matter, coupled with one elongated scene of male nudity, produced little attention, mixed reviews and only a brief run, which was followed immediately by a national touring company that crisscrossed the country playing to large and enthusiastic audiences. The production generated just enough controversy to create box-office success everywhere it went. Throughout the New York run and the United States tour, producer and director Ken Baker was present at every performance.

In mid-October 1990, the company played an engagement at the Leighton Opera House in Leighton, Tennessee. The production played twice on a Saturday night to capacity audiences. It was the first time since the newly remodeled Opera House had opened early in 1980 that two performances on the same night had been sold out.

Among the 3,200 audience members were six local police detectives, and about 1:10 a.m., following the second performance, they arrested all eleven cast members in the play, charging them under local ordinance no. 15-27, which prohibited indecent, lewd or obscene behavior and indecent exposure in public. The law also prohibited "bawdy, lewd or obscene words" and "indecent proposals, either by word or gesture."

Never before had such an arrest been made in Leighton, and while the legality of *Night Fires* had been a heated topic of controversy within the community for several weeks, the decision to make arrests was apparently made in the absence of top city officials. Police officers assigned to the Opera House used their own judgment in the matter.

When asked if he thought the play was pornographic, Detective Bruce Davis, serving as a spokesman for the arresting officers, responded, "I did, yeah. I sure did. I don't think we've got any place for that in this town. The sex and the nudity didn't bother me as much as the language. They really tore up the King's English."

"They can call it art if they want to," Davis continued, "but I call it vulgar."

Ken Baker was quick to respond. "This is crazy. The actors will be vigorously defended. We will look into every possible violation of civil rights. We will seek massive damages under both federal and Tennessee law."

Background

Perhaps not surprisingly, the controversy began some time earlier than the actual arrests, as early as the first announcement that *Night Fires* would appear in Leighton. Mayor Patti Paul had questioned at an Urban County Council meeting whether the play should appear. She voiced concern that it might violate local obscenity ordinances, and argued that the Civic Center, operator of the Opera House, and the Urban County Council should, therefore, prohibit its presentation. The problems of prior censorship, however, and a signed contract, plus a standard contractual promise from the producer that everything in the play was legal, caused the council not to take action.

County Attorney B. Bertram Bugle, Chief of Police Alan Jeans, and Public Safety Commissioner Lionel Campbell soon announced that they, too, would consider the situation, and Christian ministers debated heatedly with civil libertarians about the issues of censorship. The most obvious result of all this public attention was a brisk advance ticket sale.

On the Friday before the Saturday performances, top law enforcement personnel met together to decide on a course of action. County Attorney Bugle offered police officials the following advice: "If they break the law, arrest them. I'm concerned about people walking around, doing things." Police Chief Jeans then issued a general order to his officers that arrests should be made if any performers violated local ordinances. Commissioner Campbell said police and representatives of the county attorney's office should decide on the scene if arrests were warranted. Among other things, he said, those officials should consider whether city ordinances prohibiting lewd behavior had been violated as part of the performance, and whether the sexual activity discussed and suggested was pornographic.

Neither Bugle, Jeans nor Campbell would attend either of the performances. "I didn't care to see it, to be frank with you," Jeans would say later. "I just had no desire to see it."

Lawyer David Anderson, however, an assistant county attorney in Bugle's office, did watch the first performance on Saturday night, to offer police a legal opinion on the production. After advising them to make no arrests, that no violations of the law had taken place, Anderson left the theatre.

Final decisions about any potential arrests were left up to the policemen on the scene. While authorities had met the day before, and while Chief Jeans would later reveal that details of the arrest operation had been fully worked out at that meeting, the official public position presented by the police was that they had no position. They did not say whether arrests would be made or, if they were, what the charges might be. This official neutrality prevailed even after the first performance. One of the officers present at the Opera House, for example, Sergeant Eric Downy of the Special Investigations Unit, said in the interim between shows, "If anything happens—and I say 'if'—it will be done after the audience clears the Opera House. The audience won't know anything has happened."

In spite of the public position that no decisions had been made, "reliable sources" had predicted that cast members would be arrested after the second show. Consequently, director-producer Baker had retained lawyers William Keesle and Robert Channel to represent the company. Cast members joked awkwardly among themselves about the probability of arrest while journalists were permitted backstage during the performances to report any action.

While the cast was performing, metro police—working from the lighting control booth located above the second balcony—documented the performances with photography, an investigative technique local officials argued was routine in such cases. They shot 250 feet of movie film, plus nearly two rolls each of color and black-and-white prints.

When the second performance ended, the officers waited until the audience had moved from the auditorium, then went backstage and announced the arrest to the six actors and five actresses.

Musicians, stagehands and Baker, along with journalists and the defense lawyers, watched. The cast was then driven away in patrol cars and confined in jail. William Keesle had arranged for their release on $100 bond each by 3:00 a.m.

News of the arrests greeted the Leighton community in the Sunday newspaper. The front page headline blared "Police Nab Eleven Sex Show Performers." By Monday, of course, more details were available. Newspaper headlines announced "Police Got Bird's-Eye Photos" and "Eleven Jailed Actors Planning to Fight Obscenity Counts." On its editorial page the *Leighton Tribune* deplored the arrests, calling the event "a disgraceful episode in the history of Leighton" and arguing that "charges against the cast members should be dismissed."

The *Tribune* asked, "Should the eleven members of the cast of *Night Fires* have been arrested Saturday night at the conclusion of their performances at the Opera House?" Then it invited comments for publication.

The resultant outpouring of public opinion filled the "Letters to the Editor" section for weeks. Initial opinion predictably ranged from "Yes, a thousand times yes; we can only keep Leighton beautiful by discouraging such garbage" to "These arrests are a terrible blow to the arts and civil liberties in this area." In fact, the *Tribune* grouped the first batch of letters under conflicting headlines which read "Such Filth Shouldn't Be Allowed in Cultural Places" and "Cast Arrests Are Blow to Arts and Civil Liberties."

Within a short time those opposed to the play and supportive of the arrests had made their case. The human body had been declared "obscene," homosexual relationships had been dismissed as "aberrant," the police had received "bravos" for eliminating "on-the-stage trash," the Opera House had been condemned, and the call to arms had been issued for decent Christians and other right-thinking citizens to unite against filth and immorality, especially if it involved sex and homosexuality.

On the other side, response proved equally sure. The

arrests were hailed as "just another demonstration of the gradual removal of the basic individual rights which our Constitution guarantees," the public attitude was ridiculed as "provincial" and "outrageous," and the arresting authorities were satirized as "wonderful and heroic" persons who "withstood two entire performances of the awful play" before stopping the "horrid, indecent acts these villainous actors tried to put over on 3,200 solid citizens."

Very few letter writers, pro or con, had seen the play.

Within a short time a Citizens for Decency league had surfaced, led by several local ministers and dedicated to stopping obscenity within the community. In a move that top officials claimed was not related to *Night Fires,* the Urban County Council hurriedly passed an ordinance prohibiting the sale of explicit sexual material in places minors could enter. Magazines like *Penthouse* and *Playboy,* even *Cosmopolitan,* disappeared from shelves virtually overnight, but police announced a three-week grace period before enforcement of the law would begin. More than four hundred persons crowded the Urban County Council chambers to encourage the law, and they cheered when it passed, rising for a minute-long standing ovation.

Meanwhile, the arts community and Leighton's various arts organizations were surprisingly silent. In fact, the first and only organized protest of the arrests came from a state theatre organization, which passed unanimously a resolution condemning the arrests and calling on local authorities to nullify their actions. The resolution stated that the "arrest and confinement of artists for pursuing their art cannot be tolerated in a free society," and it was released to media in the city and state.

While the public controversy grew more and more heated, the legal battle also continued. When the case was first called in Quarterly Court, Keesle pled his defendants "not guilty" and requested a three-week postponement of the case. He also announced that the central issue in defense of cast members would be the constitutionality of the city ordinance under which they had been arrested.

The ordinance in question had already been ruled unconstitutional in at least one earlier case, because of its vague wording. Keesle had also been the defense attorney in that case. As one local attorney explained, however, such a ruling "from the lowest court in the state" does not constitute an "ultimate and final" test of the law, nor does it require city officials to remove or rewrite the ordinance. Therefore, the law was still on the books.

Director-producer Baker, also an attorney, responded to questions about the proposed defense position by saying, "We will have as much difficulty in proving that ordinance unconstitutional as your local university would have in defeating a local high school in a basketball scrimmage." Baker also referred to the arrests as "a little taste of your Southern hospitality," and wondered why, "if we had done something wrong in the first show, they didn't come to us and say so," rather than waiting until after the second performance to take action.

The judge, responding to the defense motion, set November 12 as the hearing date for the case.

At noon on the twelfth, a group of twenty persons protested the arrests outside the Municipal Building, carrying signs such as "Obscenity Is in the Mind of the Beholder." When questioned, one of the group expressed concern that treatment of the *Night Fires* cast would cause Leighton to be "blacklisted" by theatre people. "Nothing's been accomplished," he said, "except damage to the arts in the city." Another demonstrator called the arrests "totally absurd," arguing that they affected only "the most innocent parties in the whole thing."

The demonstrators dispersed about 1:00 p.m., but were soon replaced by a second group, equally small, who supported the arrests. The new demonstrators, led by local ministers, carried protest signs as "The Opera House Was Built for Class, not Crass"; most of those who gathered had also protested outside the Opera House on the night of the performances.

Unbeknownst to either group, earlier in the day a judge had postponed any ruling on the obscenity charges, and a new hearing date had been set for December 10. Quarterly Court Trial Commissioner Michael J. Deacon had signed the postponement order after agreeing to hear arguments before ruling on a defense motion for dismissal because the ordinance under which the cast had been charged had already been ruled unconstitutional. Deacon gave attorneys until a week before the hearing to submit briefs, with the exception voiced that he would decide the guilt or innocence of the eleven arrested performers on December 10, if the case were not dismissed.

On December 10, the case was again postponed. On December 20, however, Deacon dismissed all charges against the cast members, ruling in a six-page written statement that the ordinance under which they had been charged was "unconstitutionally vague." Deacon held that the ordinance failed to set specific standards for obscenity, a requirement established by the U.S. Supreme Court. "By stating simply that any 'indecent, lewd or obscene act' committed in public will lead to criminal prosecution," Deacon argued, "the ordinance fails in every way to meet the requirements" outlined by the Supreme Court.

Deacon included in his opinion that "it should be made abundantly clear . . . that this decision is in no way an endorsement of any activity of the kind allegedly committed by these defendants." Because the issue concerned the constitutionality of the law itself, Deacon did not rule regarding the guilt or innocence of the cast members. He did say: "In view of the unparalleled publicity and public response generated by this case, there will undoubtedly be those who misconstrue the decision which is reached here today. It bears repeating, then, that conduct of the type alleged of these defendants may properly be prohibited by local law, but only if that law defines the specifics under which the conduct of all persons will be judged."

The charges had been dismissed. The cast was free.

Aftermath

Response to Deacon's decision varied.

Director Baker called it "not unexpected. We have been in litigation in a number of cities in the United States—and we can now include Leighton in the United States."

County Attorney Bugle said he had "no reaction at all, because the court has spoken."

Michael Foster, Leighton's deputy mayor, was "not surprised," and vowed the city would consider immediately whether to appeal the decision. Foster had earlier indicated that he was "amused and surprised" by the arrests, saying he would have advised against such action.

The *Leighton Tribune,* which throughout had maintained a strong editorial position, hailed Deacon's decision, calling for "a sincere apology from the public officials who had a hand in this sorry episode." The Reverend Bruce Daniels, a member of the Citizens for Decency and part of a group of about ten persons who demonstrated outside the courtroom at the time Deacon's decision was handed down, said the judge's decision seemed "proper." He added, however, that they were present "to encourage the conviction of the *Night Fires* actresses and actors if you can call them that," and even though the charges had been dismissed, "as far as the cast's guilt on indecency and lewdness, there is no doubt they're guilty."

More than two months of legal deliberations and public controversy had ended. But the passions raised remained undiminished, and the focus of public attention on issues of censorship was far from over.

On the day that Deacon dismissed the charges on *Night Fires,* twelve books (including the best-seller, *The Joy of Sex*) were confiscated from three Leighton bookstores in the police department's first enforcement of the new "anti-smut" ordinance. Leighton's single adult bookstore was not involved, and each of the three bookstores cited belonged to national chains. The arrests were made without warning, without consultation by high-level officials, and without warrants. They were based on a single anonymous complaint to police.

The cycle was to begin again.

Baker's evaluation

Producer-director Ken Baker, after the charges were dismissed, was invited by the Leighton University Department of Theatre (which had remained silent throughout the entire controversy) to meet with faculty and students to discuss the incident. Rather than recount details of the episode, Baker shared ten specific observations with the audience of two hundred that gathered to hear him talk. "The result of all this, beyond the dismissal of charges, is difficult to assess," he said. "But several conclusions need to be drawn, even if they are tentative at this point." Then he outlined ten issues:

1. The public outcry before and after the *Night Fires* performances, the continuing "anti-pornography" campaign, the tone of Trial Commissioner Deacon's decision—all reaffirm once again that censorship in the arts is more a matter of social conviction than of law. Ultimate victory, even when tempered by court decisions to the contrary, frequently belongs to those with the loudest and most persistent voices. In Leighton, the cast members of *Night Fires* have been freed (if not found innocent), but books and magazines have vanished from bookstores, and insidious fear of repression—real or imagined—reigns. Even the public library has been checking its shelves to see if "objectionable" material should be removed.

2. The "unparalleled" public concern cited by Deacon and obvious in the media suggests that public opinion concerning "obscenity" and "pornography" is as highly polarized as ever. Reason, it should be remembered, frequently plays only a small, insignificant role in the polarization, and the conflict is often falsely dramatized as being between the Bible and the U.S. Constitution.

3. The indirect effects of censorship can be more bitter than the direct outcome of any specific confrontation. In Leighton, for example, a downtown church has now used its influence—without overt action—to discourage renewal of the Opera House liquor license. A state law in Tennessee provides that any establishment seeking to serve liquor within two hundred feet of a church must have the church's written approval. When a church near the Opera House threatened to revoke its approval, the Opera House, rather than risk confrontation less than two weeks after the arrests, chose not to apply for renewal.

4. The arts community, if it cares for the freedoms guaranteed by the Constitution, must speak out in defense of those freedoms, sure in the knowledge that it will not always be able to choose just what to defend. Rarely are the issues of censorship both just and popular. Rarely are they polite.

Rarely do they provoke feelings of goodwill. As the *Leighton Tribune* pointed out four days after the arrests, "One does not have to approve of *Night Fires* to defend its right to be performed. The artistic merit of the sexual material is debatable. But it is not the business of the police or any other government agency to squelch or inhibit that debate."

5. The long-range effects of a censorship confrontation may be as important as the outcome of short-range specific situations. What play won't be staged in Leighton now because of subtle fear?

6. The enforcement of censorship laws—will it ever be different?—is frequently a political rather than a legal matter. The *Night Fires* cast was arrested on October 15. The "anti-smut" ordinance was passed on November 3. The Tennessee general election was held on November 8. Interestingly enough, each of the highly visible public officials in the incident was running for re-election. Equally interesting, each was running unopposed.

7. The "it can't happen here" defense for indifference remains foolhardy, if not downright stupid. It can happen anywhere.

8. Public opinion in the United States sooner or later becomes political reality. And theatres, together with other arts organizations, have a primary responsibility for helping to shape public opinion. One Tennessee theatre group took a first step in its resolution of condemnation. What else might it have done? What should it have done prior to the incident? What should it and other arts organizations be doing now?

9. Theatre, like all the arts, if it is vigorous, will frequently be controversial. Vigor is not guaranteed by controversy, nor is controversy a sign of vigor, but the two often cohabit. Therefore, to encourage vigor is to invite controversy. And controversy frequently arrives with suppression as its partner.

10. The Boy Scouts have the right idea: be prepared.

Questions

1. What are the major problems, if any, in this case? What, if anything, could have been done to prevent them? Should Baker have done anything differently?

2. Analyze Baker's ten observations. Are there ideas you would add to his list?

3. What responsibilities, if any, does a director owe to controversy?

Note: This case is adapted freely from an article written by J. Robert Wills. Titled "Censorship in the Arts," it appeared in *Southern Theatre* (Summer 1978).

CASE 41. ETHICS: *HAMLET*

Laura Delaney, a young, third-year faculty member without tenure at Wilpauto University, knew that her chairman, William Deager, was a demanding, relentless and seemingly brilliant artist and administrator who had built theatre at Wilpauto over the years into a program of considerable size, strength and reputation. Deager tried to employ faculty and staff—and there were nineteen of them in all—who shared his single-minded desire to create an academic and artistic program of distinction. Delaney liked working with and for him. In turn, Deager seemed to respond well to Delaney's efforts.

The newest member of the directing staff, Delaney had been assigned by Deager to direct *Hamlet,* an obviously ambitious undertaking and only her second production at Wilpauto. On the morning of the day of auditions, Deager stopped Delaney in the hallway to say that his son, Michael, would be auditioning for the production. "I know," he said, "that Michael is only a first-year student, but he seems perfect for the role of Horatio, the friend of Hamlet. That would be a good way for him to begin his career here at Wilpauto. And casting him," Deager continued with a laugh, "wouldn't hurt at all your chances for tenure next year." Deager walked away from her, and disappeared into his office.

"What should I do?" Delaney thought later. "If I refuse to accept Deager's suggestion, if I don't cast Michael as Horatio, what will my future be at Wilpauto? What will happen if I cast Michael in some role other than Horatio? Or, worse yet, what will happen if I don't cast him at all? Then, if I actually accept Deager's suggestion and cast Michael as Horatio, how will I live with myself?"

Questions

1. What should Delaney do?

2. What would you do in similar circumstances?

CASE 42. CODE OF ETHICS: ELIPSE CONTEMPORARY THEATRE

Janice Christopher had applied for the position of Artistic Director with the Elipse Contemporary Theatre, a five-year-old professional theatre in Minneapolis that in only a few short years had already developed an outstanding record in the nurturing of new scripts. Christopher, too, had an outstanding record in the Twin Cities, having worked successfully for a decade as a free-lance director while she also pursued a developing career in sculpture. Board members of the Elipse Theatre had interviewed her as one of three final candidates for the position, which involved directing four of the eight plays in the Elipse season and serving as producer for all Elipse production activity. After a week, the interview committee had invited Christopher to return for a second interview. John McAdams, the elected board president and chairman of the Artistic Director Search Committee, had been specific in his communication with her: "This second interview will focus especially on what we have been calling the director's code of ethics. We would like to talk about those ethical considerations which would govern your work— and by your work, we mean specifically your work as the director of individual plays, not necessarily your work as Artistic Director of the Theatre. Please bring some written ideas for what you think is important," McAdams had concluded, "and we'll use that as a place to begin."

Now Christopher sat near the middle of the bus, riding downtown to meet with the interview committee. She read again the notes she had developed. After careful thought, she had written fifteen simple statements that seemed to summarize her ethical beliefs. Writing them down had not been easy, and as the time for her interview grew nearer, she wondered whether the list was complete enough. She also wondered whether it really dealt with the ethical values she thought were important for a director. Her list read as follows:

Code of Ethics: The Director
1. The director should communicate frankly, honestly and straightforwardly.

2. The director should bear criticism gracefully.

3. The director should recognize the importance of moral, ethical and professional integrity before, during and after the production process.

4. The director should not seek special favor with critics.

5. The director should not discriminate against any person on the basis of sex, race, religious belief or political affiliation.

6. The director should insure that co-artists and collaborators receive proper credit and recognition for their work.

7. The director should respect confidences, and insure that artistic colleagues also respect confidences.

8. The director should endorse full freedom of expression.

9. The director should be honest.

10. The director should treat others with respect.

11. The director should cast plays through open auditions, without precasting, without prejudice and without prior selection by any means, unless deviation from openness has been announced in a public manner prior to auditions.

12. The director should be sure that the appropriate royalties are paid.

13. The director should adhere to the spirit of truth in the material presented.

14. The director should establish positive relationships with other artists and with the community.

15. The director should establish positive relationships with all people active in the Elipse Theatre, from board officers to audience members.

Questions

1. Analyze Christopher's Code of Ethics for the director.

2. What additional items would you add to the list? Why? Are there individual items you would remove from the list? Why?

3. What role should ethics play in the work of a director?

Note: Items 4, 5, 9, and 13 are drawn from the Code of Ethics first devised by the former American Theatre Association.

CASE 43. GENDER IN CASTING: *WAITING FOR GODOT*

Deane Gale had been selected to direct Samuel Beckett's *Waiting for Godot* as a Second Season production at the University of Iola. While not part of the main subscription series, plays in the Second Season were fully produced and were presented for twelve public performances in the 400-seat Almond Theatre. Gale knew that the characters in the play—Vladimir, Estragon, Lucky, Pozzo and a Boy—had been written to be played by male actors, but she wanted instead to cast women in each of the five roles.

Knowing that she might have to secure permission of some sort to make this kind of change in a Beckett play, she was nonetheless ready to argue that nothing in the life of the text was limited only to men, and that a switch in gender for the various roles would add a richness to the play while providing the audience with a deep, if different, experience. Furthermore, Gale could find no place in the writing where gender, as such, was an issue. She knew, however, that it would become an issue if she cast women.

Questions

1. What do you think about the casting that Gale is considering?

2. What, in general, do you think about changing gender in casting? In plays or characters where gender is of little or no importance? In plays where gender is of considerable or central importance?

3. Would a director need to seek permission from a publisher or playwright to make gender changes in casting?

CASE 44. BEYOND TRADITION: NORTHERN STATE UNIVERSITY

Director Torg Anderson sat with a copy of *Beyond Tradition*[1] on the desk before him. Edited by Clinton Turner Davis and Harry Newman, the book included transcripts from the "First National Symposium on Non-Traditional Casting," a two-day conference held at the Shubert Theatre in New York City in November 1986 that would later be called "the first open discussion of the under-representation and misrepresentation of ethnic artists in the performing arts." Anderson knew that non-traditional casting, in addition to ethnic artists, also involved women and actors with disabilities. In fact, Anderson had learned that the Non-Traditional Casting Project of Actors' Equity defined non-traditional casting as "the casting of ethnic, female or disabled actors in roles where race, ethnicity, gender or physical capability are not necessary to the characters' or play's development."

Anderson had attended the 1986 New York symposium as the Director of Theatre for Northern State University, and since then he had come to believe that his own directing could benefit from such an approach to casting. Consequently, he had begun actively seeking non-traditional casts for each of the two productions he directed every year at Northern. His audition notices now said, "The director of this production actively seeks a multi-ethnic, multi-abled cast, and encourages all persons interested in acting to audition." In addition, his printed playbills now included the following notation: "Except in roles where race, gender, physical ability or ethnicity are important, casting for this production has been based on ability and talent alone." In these ways, he thought, both actors and audience members would have some knowledge of his casting and production philosophy.

The results of Anderson's efforts had been rewarding to him. Several ethnic actors had auditioned for the first time at Northern, and they had been cast in roles of significance, playing them well. A sophomore student who used a wheelchair had even auditioned, and had proved a valuable addition to the acting company. Most audience members had seemed openly receptive to such casting, although—to be sure—a vocal segment were not. In like manner, most of Anderson's colleagues in the Theatre Department supported his efforts. But not all did.

Now Anderson wanted to extend his own practice so that it could become departmental policy—for every director and every play. He had discussed this idea with several departmental committees, including the Production Committee, and he had talked with both graduate and undergraduate students. As a result of his preliminary work, he had called a special department meeting of all faculty and students to discuss the implications of initiating such a policy—and to discuss a proposed policy itself. He had promised to draft the necessary materials for presentation at the meeting.

Background

Northern State University was one of the two primary research universities in the state, and it had a large theatre operation which enjoyed an enviable national reputation. Offering the B.A, B.F.A., M.A., M.F.A. and Ph.D. degrees, the theatre program enrolled more than 300 undergraduate majors and some 120 graduate students. Specializations included acting, directing, theatre history and theory, design and production, playwriting, children's theatre and creative drama, performance art, and dance. Anderson served as chair of the department as well as Director of Theatre, but the administrative and artistic affairs of the program were handled primarily by a number of very strong and active faculty-student committees. Of these, the Production Committee was easily the most influential. Charged with recommending policies, personnel and specific plays for production, the Production Committee virtually controlled Northern's production activity, even though its recommendations went regularly to the entire faculty and staff of thirty-three for review and final approval.

Northern sponsored an ambitious annual production season that usually had six individual parts: the Subscription Season of eight productions; the Thesis Season of ten to twelve M.F.A. productions; the Children's Theatre series of four productions; a statewide touring production; a three-concert dance season; and a series of informal presentations, primarily one-acts, presented every Tuesday afternoon throughout the year. Faculty and students alike acted, directed and designed in each of the different series.

The majority of participants in this active program—faculty, staff and students—were Caucasian. Indeed, Northern's entire non-white population, out of 30,000 students, was only 2,800 students. In addition, there were some 250 students with disabilities. Among the theatre faculty, one dancer and one acting teacher were African-American; one lighting designer was Hispanic; one theatre historian was Asian. Anderson and the others were Caucasian. Only three faculty members were women—two dancers and a theatre historian. Among the theatre students, more than half were women, three or four were African-American, seven were Hispanic, two were Asian-Americans. There were no Native Americans in the theatre program.

Anderson's introduction of non-traditional casting had been widely if not unanimously accepted at Northern, especially among women and ethnic minorities. Students seemed more open to the changes involved than faculty, but almost everyone who was willing to express an opinion agreed with Harry Newman, Executive Director of the Non-Traditional Casting Project, when he said that non-traditional casting might have "become something of a buzz word" in theatre, but at the same time, it had also provided at least beginning opportunity for previously disenfranchised actors to perform—and to perform in roles of importance. Those who supported the idea, Anderson knew, also agreed with Alan Eisenberg, the Executive Secretary of Actors' Equity, that non-traditional casting was nothing more or less than "an act of artistic good sense," since it involved casting the best-qualified performers without regard for skin color, gender or physical ability, thereby enlarging the available talent pool.

Anderson also knew that the acceptance of non-traditional casting was by no means universal. Some saw it as only a ploy to use theatre for social goals. Others argued that audiences just wouldn't accept such deviation from the "norm." Still others brought forth such arguments as historical accuracy and the perceived intention of playwrights, especially classic playwrights. Anderson felt that there might be some unstated reasons, as well, that had yet to surface in any meaningful way. What this meant, of course—and Anderson wondered about the magnitude of his suspicions in this regard—was that sexism and racism, whether overt or subtle, were likely participants in the arguments for or against non-traditional casting.

Among the national voices opposed to non-traditional casting, none had been stronger than John Simon, theatre critic for *New York* magazine. Simon had written that non-traditional casting was "biologically preposterous" and "socially inconceivable."[2] Non-traditional casting, he argued, "is the equivalent of affirmative action in the theatre, which stipulates that companies unable to survive without subsidies can get them only by casting persons of color, of the wrong gender, with physical handicaps, etc., in parts for which they are totally unsuited. It means defying logic, historical and social authenticity, and biological credibility, thus making the theatre a political battleground at the expense of artistic integrity and efficacy." Furthermore, according to Simon, "untalented directors . . . use 'good citizenship' to cover up their bad workmanship . . . as further means of deflecting attention from their basic incompetence."[3]

Anderson knew that several in the Northern audience agreed with Simon. In addition, perhaps as many as five faculty members would also openly argue Simon's position. Would there be silent agreement, as well, he wondered, among other faculty and students?

The Anderson plan

Anderson's plan seemed simple enough to him. First, he wanted Northern's Department of Theatre and Dance to embrace formally the general idea of non-traditional casting. Then, he wanted the department to adopt a policy that would address specifically how that general idea would be put into action. Finally, he hoped the department would devise a means by which this new policy could be actively and aggressively implemented. Adoption of this three-part plan would, Anderson thought, enhance the theatre's potential artistic excellence, and this was the most compelling reason in his mind for taking such action. But he also thought that adoption of the plan could enable Northern's theatre to become a leader of society as well as a "mirror of nature," while also placing the theatre in a position of saying publicly, "What is right is right!"

As for the specific policy he wanted to propose, Anderson knew that some theatres had tried to do a once-a-year ethnic production or a once-a-year play which featured women, but he had rejected this notion as actually limiting experience, perpetuating separatism and leaving many actors outside the mainstream. Anderson had also considered, then rejected, the possibility of just issuing a statement that all casting at Northern would be "blind casting," casting that ignored differences which might exist among actors. Such a general policy, he thought, would make no one specifically responsible for any change and would leave people too free to pursue whatever their past practices had been.

Instead, Anderson had searched for a policy which could be active rather than passive, which could express not just a willingness to accept non-traditional casting, but an aggressive pursuit of it. At the end of his search, he had decided to propose a policy first suggested by a theatre colleague at another university, a policy which would place the burden of responsibility on individual directors and on the specific selection of individual plays to be directed. Anderson wanted nothing less than a departmental commitment to the idea that directors at Northern, whether faculty or students, would direct only those plays in which they could cast woman actors, disabled actors and ethnic actors in meaningful roles.[4] He envisioned a procedure by which directors actually signed a statement before directing assignments were made final, a statement which might read: "In choosing to direct this play, I plan that casting for the production will be open to women actors, disabled actors and ethnic actors—to all who might audition."

Anderson knew that the adoption of such a policy would eliminate the possibility of some plays for some directors. One director might be able to consider, for example, directing *Death of a Salesman* under such circumstances; another might not. Anderson also thought that adoption of such a policy might eliminate some plays from production entirely. But he felt strongly that only by adopting such a policy would the entire department be influenced by the desired casting goal.

Anderson had heard that a few among the faculty might suggest to the department that it should adopt three policies, not just one. He was told that these colleagues would argue that the circumstances surrounding the casting of women, ethnic minorities and persons with disabilities were so completely different that each demanded a separate policy.

Regardless of the specific policy or policies eventually adopted by the department, Anderson also wanted the theatre to adopt a plan for implementing the policy, a plan that would have eight specific steps.[5] He had prepared a brief, informal description of these steps for distribution and action at the meeting:

1. We must develop a *written* policy. Writing things down helps make them real. And the policy should include clear expectations supported by a clear rationale. It should also be formally approved by the department and it should provide for whatever exceptions we might want to include.

2. We must develop a grievance procedure that encourages students and others to "make noise" if they think the written policy isn't being followed. This grievance procedure should begin informally somehow, but should also provide for formal inquiry when necessary. The policy must be "user friendly."

3. We must distribute the policy widely. It cannot be a secret policy or a secret document. We should publish it in our catalogs, brochures, playbills, audition notices, cast lists, handbooks—in everything we print. We should also be especially certain that *new* faculty, staff and students know about it.

4. We should teach the policy in class—in every class, during every semester. We should regularly explore both the rationale for and the implementation of our policy.

5. We should appoint a coordinator for the policy. Someone must be in charge, must hold all the rest of us

accountable, and it should be one of our respected colleagues who has a real commitment to the policy itself.

6. We should publish the results of our policy at least once a year. How are we doing, we should ask. Can we brag? Do we need to do better?

7. We should use the policy actively in the recruitment of students, faculty and staff. There are opportunities here for us to expand the diversity of our population.

8. We should evaluate the policy regularly. Is it working? Should it be changed in any way?

As Anderson prepared for the departmental meeting, he knew that some people would support his ideas and that others would not. But he looked forward to the discussion, and he hoped the result would be a department that embraced a policy of non-traditional casting.

Questions

1. Are the ideas that Anderson proposes wise? Why or why not?

2. Analyze Anderson's specific idea for a departmental policy statement. Should each director be asked to agree to such a statement?

3. Analyze Anderson's eight-point plan for implementing a non-traditional casting policy. What would you add or subtract from his list?

4. What advice would you give Anderson as he prepares for the forthcoming meeting?

5. If the department were to adopt Anderson's ideas, what would you recommend, if anything, concerning the possible "education" of the Northern theatre audience?

Notes
[1]*Beyond Tradition* is published by the Non-Traditional Casting Project, Inc., P.O. Box 6443, Grand Central Station, New

York, NY 10163-6021. The quoted materials in this case are drawn from this publication. This case is intended only for classroom discussion.

[2]*New York,* April 8, 1991, p. 96.

[3]*New York,* March 11, 1991, p. 90.

[4]This idea was first suggested to me by Patti Gillespie, who now teaches at the University of Maryland, College Park, MD, and who wrote about the idea in "Actor's Equity: The Problems of Casting," *ACA Bulletin* (1981).

[5]Anderson's eight steps have been guided in content by the sexual harassment policies of the American Council of Education, One Dupont Circle, Washington, DC 20036.

CASE 45. DEALING WITH THE PUBLIC:
THE MERCHANT OF VENICE

Cynthia Felderstein sat quietly behind the long, draped table placed center stage in the small lecture hall on the Central State University campus in Colorado. To her left sat Suzannah Keel, to her right, Brian Klas. Both were Shakespearean scholars from California. Felderstein was a director. Her production of *The Merchant of Venice* had opened less than a week earlier at the Flat Rock Summer Festival Theatre. Together, Keel, Klas and Felderstein were ready to respond to audience questions and participate in a discussion about the play and the production.

Only forty or fifty people crowded into the small hall, but they filled the aisles and stairs as well as the available seats. Felderstein guessed that about half the audience was angry. The remainder seemed divided between the curious and those eager to hear the announced discussion. By and large, she thought, the angry audience members were "locals"; the rest were mostly tourists, in town for theatre and a few days of vacation. She was less than a minute away from beginning her remarks to the audience, but as the crowd settled down, she still didn't know for sure just how she would begin. Never before had the theatre scheduled such a discussion.

Background

The Flat Rock Summer Festival Theatre had been in operation for almost two decades. It began as a company of nine young theatre professionals who presented three plays in July and August on the shallow stage of a rented movie theatre. It had grown to a full company of actors, designers, technicians, administrators, interns and others who presented a season of fourteen plays, usually drawn from the classic repertoire. The annual budget had grown from $12,000 to $3 million. The theatre drew an audience from throughout the United States. Indeed, it had become a vacation attraction of some importance to the state and regional economies, and it now performed plays from mid-April to late September each year in its own building complex, which housed three different

197

theatres and all the necessary support space for a major producing theatre.

Felderstein's production of *The Merchant of Venice* had opened without fanfare and was scheduled to run every night for three weeks. The morning after opening, however, Isaac Zactow, a rabbi from Santa Fe called Flat Rock's Artistic Director, Douglas Berner, to insist that the character of Shylock be changed to something that would—in his mind— be less of an anti-Semitic stereotype. Zactow said that many local Jews, and many tourists, were offended by the portrayal of Shakespeare's Jewish moneylender, who seeks his "pound of flesh" from the merchant Antonio.

"It is the modern director's duty," said Zactow, "to direct the play so as to bring out Shylock's most noble qualities. Especially now, after the Holocaust, the director must underplay the problem inherent in the script. Don't change any words," Zactow continued, "just play down all the objectionable things."

Berner dismissed Zactow's comments at first as a "tempest in a teapot," but by mid-afternoon he had received twenty-three additional calls, all saying similar things. The evening newspaper, whose first edition appeared about 3:00 p.m., carried a full, front-page story about Zactow's concerns. (The review of the production, which appeared on page 8, did not mention any concern, and generally praised the opening performance.) Soon after, the local television station appeared to film Berner making a short statement. "We will not change the production," he said. "I think the main objection must be that we've reset the piece in modern times. It seems far more painful and more direct, evidently, to have people hurl catcalls at Shylock when it's done in the 1990's."

Later, when the same film crew taped Zactow, he said, "I have no objection whatsoever to the modern dress or to setting the play in modern times. But I do object to lots of other things. Why," he said, "should Shylock be costumed in a suit and tie with a yarmulke on his head? This desecrates Jewish symbols and must be stopped. By emphasizing the character's religion, the director and the actor are merely emphasizing the stereotype. The play by itself is bad enough. Why add fuel to the fire?"

Rabbi Daniel Berniker of Beth El Temple in Flat Rock said the next day on the local radio station that he and other Jews in Flat Rock were, indeed, upset by the production. "I personally found the performance flawed," he said, "and less sympathetic in its portrayal of Shylock than other productions I've seen. But I disagree with Rabbi Zactow when he claims the play desecrates our Jewish religious symbols. Besides," Berniker concluded, "this is Flat Rock, not Nazi Germany."

The disagreement continued all week—in the press, on the airwaves, and in the theatre lobby, where conversation among audience members often seemed to focus on nothing else.

By the third performance, on Thursday, Berner had announced the open discussion, to be held Sunday. He quickly contacted Keel and Klas, then asked Felderstein to lead the public conversation, which he hoped she would begin with a very brief, two- or three-minute statement, to be followed immediately by comments and questions from the audience. All three panel members would respond, Berner hoped, as it seemed appropriate, and would also have some interaction among themselves.

Felderstein checked her watch one last time, gauging the gathering crowd. Should she defend her artistic decisions in the opening remarks? Should she point out the differing opinions which had emerged about the production? Should she say nothing at all, and just begin? Should she begin in some other way? The moment for decision was arriving, and as she invited the audience to be quiet, she noticed Zactow and Berniker sitting together in the front row.

Questions

1. Analyze this situation. What are the problems suggested, if any? Has the Flat Rock Summer Festival Theatre handled them effectively?

2. What advice would you give Felderstein about the open discussion and her opening remarks?

3. What should Berner and Felderstein do, if anything, during the next two weeks?

Note: This brief has been prepared from reports published in April 1990, by the Associated Press. Names, locations and other details have been altered in the writing. In its present form, the brief is intended only for classroom use.

CASE 46. SECOND-NIGHT BLUES:
DEATH OF A SALESMAN

John Richter knew that his Alcorn College production of Arthur Miller's *Death of a Salesman* would be fine; Alcorn had a long tradition in theatre, talented students and an excellent production facility. Indeed, the *Salesman* cast was rehearsing well, growing nicely; outwardly everything seemed to be falling into place effectively.

Richter also knew, however, that if past experience held true, the production would "peak" for opening night, then suffer a debilitating letdown for the second performance, before settling into a fairly consistent and maturing run. This phenomenon, the "second-night letdown," seemed to affect every Alcorn production, and Richter wondered whether he could change that pattern with *Death of a Salesman*.

Question

1. What should Richter do to avoid this problem?

CASE 47. EVALUATING THE DIRECTOR: SABANA UNIVERSITY

"Judgments about directorial effectiveness frequently rely more on subjective than on objective criteria. Written critical reviews, analysis of audience response, formal sessions of oral criticism, informal comments, hallway talk, the observed artistic growth of actors, the welcome and not-so-welcome observations of colleagues—all can lead to highly subjective notions of effectiveness. Furthermore, the overall sense of a performance often outweighs its individual elements, which may be desirable for an audience, but actually blurs areas of concern for the director, making it difficult to identify specific strengths and weaknesses."

Student Elizabeth Wood read these notes from her last directing class at Sabana University and realized that her assignment was due in less than an hour. Professor Roger West had asked her to create an assessment form for directors, something—he said—that would stimulate classroom discussion about how best to evaluate a director's work. He believed that to improve their effectiveness, directors, while very much concerned with overall results, needed to concentrate on particular areas of both the process and the product of their work.

Consequently, Wood had devised two forms to help focus attention on just such concerns. The first she designed primarily for use by actors in evaluating the director of a production in which they had been cast. The second she designed primarily to be used by knowledgeable audience members following a given performance. Neither form, she knew, would provide a truly objective measure of effectiveness, but she did think that each might reveal useful and valuable perceptions. Now she reviewed the forms one last time before leaving for class. (The two forms can be found in Appendices I and II, following.)

Questions

1. Analyze both of Wood's forms as a means for assessing a director's effectiveness.

2. What items would you add to each of her forms in order to make it more useful?

3. What other ideas do you have for implementing a formal evaluation process for directors?

Note: These evaluation forms and the introduction to them first appeared, in somewhat different form, in *The Director in a Changing Theatre,* edited by J. Robert Wills (Palo Alto, CA, 1976).

CASE 47. APPENDIX I

EVALUATION FORM A

Indicate your response to each item by circling the number which most clearly expresses your considered opinion.

$$5 = \text{Outstanding}$$
$$4 = \text{Above average}$$
$$3 = \text{Average}$$
$$2 = \text{Below average}$$
$$1 = \text{Poor}$$

Title of play_____

Name of director_____

A. ABOUT THE DIRECTOR

1.	Knowledge of directing	1	2	3	4	5
2.	Skill in directing	3	2	1	4	5
3.	Preparation for production	5	2	1	3	4
4.	Communication with actors	2	3	4	5	1
5.	Concern for the audience	2	5	3	1	4
6.	Interest in the production	5	4	3	2	1
7.	Level of creativity	3	4	2	1	5
8.	Organization	2	5	4	1	3
9.	Ability to stimulate actors	4	1	5	3	2
10.	Openness to disagreement	1	2	5	3	4
11.	Attitude toward actors	5	4	1	2	3
12.	Sense of humor	1	5	4	3	2
13.	Working relationships with co-artists other than actors	2	4	5	3	1
14.	Efficiency	3	5	4	1	2
15.	Level of expectation	5	4	3	1	2
16.	Punctuality	2	1	4	3	5
17.	Helpfulness to you as an actor	3	2	5	1	4
18.	Patience	2	4	1	3	5
19.	Concern for the total production	5	2	3	1	4
20.	Overall effectiveness	4	3	1	2	5
21.	Understanding of the script	5	4	3	1	2
22.	Understanding of actors	3	1	2	4	5

23. Understanding of the technical
    aspects of production   5 4 1 2 3
24. Encouragement of production
    growth   2 5 3 4 1
25. Handling of human problems   4 1 3 5 2
26. Try-out procedures   1 5 2 4 3
27. The level of creativity expected of
    you   4 3 1 5 2

B. ABOUT YOU
1. Your enthusiasm for rehearsal   1 2 3 4 5
2. Your enthusiasm for performance   5 4 1 3 2
3. Your concentration in rehearsal   2 1 5 4 3
4. Your preparation for rehearsal   3 5 4 2 1
5. Your punctuality   4 2 3 1 5
6. Your artistic growth through
   rehearsal and performance   5 1 3 2 4
7. Your growth in the crafts or skills of
   acting   3 2 4 5 1
8. Your growth in knowledge of and
   appreciation for theatre   1 5 4 3 2
9. Your overall effort   2 3 5 1 4
10. Your overall results   3 5 4 2 1

C. ABOUT REHEARSAL
1. The atmosphere of rehearsals   1 3 2 5 4
2. The efficiency of rehearsal periods   2 1 5 3 4
3. The scheduling of rehearsals   4 5 1 2 3
4. Working relationship between actor
   and director during rehearsals   3 4 5 1 2
5. The growth which took place during
   rehearsals   2 3 4 5 1

D. ABOUT THE PERFORMANCE
1. Quality of the performance   5 4 2 3 1
2. Quality of the finished production   1 4 2 3 5
3. Quality of directing   2 5 4 3 1
4. Sense of ensemble   3 4 2 1 5
5. Quality of acting   4 1 3 2 5
6. Sense of theatrical unity   2 1 5 4 3

7. Audience appreciation of and
   involvement with performance   4 2 1 5 3
8. Your *awareness* of audience response   3 5 2 1 4
9. Your *concern* for audience response   3 2 1 5 4

E. GENERAL
1. Compared to all theatre experiences
    you have had, how would you rate this
    experience?   2 1 5 4 3
2. Compared to all directors you have
    known, how would you rate this
    director   5 4 2 3 1

Other comments:

Case 47. Appendix II

EVALUATION FORM B

Please circle the appropriate response, leaving blank any items not applicable:

    5 = Outstanding
    4 = Above average
    3 = Average
    2 = Below average
    1 = Poor

Understanding of text	1 2 3 4 5
Casting	1 2 1 4 5
Acting	5 2 1 3 4
Movement	2 3 4 5 1
Picturization	2 5 3 1 4
Use of stage areas	5 4 3 2 1
Use of body position	3 4 2 1 5
Use of level	2 5 4 1 3
Use of plane	4 1 5 3 2
Emphasis	1 2 5 3 4
Focus	5 4 1 2 3
Business	1 5 4 3 2
Rhythm	2 4 5 3 1
Tempo	3 5 4 1 2
Ground plan	5 4 3 1 2
Mood	2 1 4 3 5
Aural effectiveness	3 2 5 1 4
Kinetic effectiveness	2 4 1 3 5
Clarity	5 2 3 1 4
Variety	4 3 1 2 5
Sense of unity	5 4 3 1 2
Overall effectiveness	3 1 2 4 5
Creativity	1 4 3 2 5

Comments:

About the Author

J. ROBERT WILLS (B.A., College of Wooster; M.A., University of Illinois; Ph.D., Case–Western Reserve University; Certificate in Arts Administration, Harvard University) is Professor of Theatre and Provost at Pacific Lutheran University in Tacoma, Washington. He has taught and directed at Wittenberg University, the University of Kentucky and the University of Texas at Austin, places where he also served at various times as theatre program director, department chair and college dean. A frequent consultant in the United States and abroad, he has directed more than ninety full-length productions, produced some four hundred plays, authored about sixty articles concerning theatre and the arts, and edited *The Director in a Changing Theatre* (Palo Alto, CA, 1976). In addition, he has served as President of the University and College Theatre Association and of the Association for Communication Administration, and as Secretary/Treasurer for the International Council of Fine Arts Deans.